Introductic

Kingswear lies on the southern tip of a penins
southwest of Torbay. The village enjoys a
facing, with the River Dart as one of its bour
opposite bank of the river. The peninsula i
River Dart as it meanders down from Dartmoor via Totnes, and to tne east anu
south by the English Channel. This geographical situation was crucial to the role
in which Kingswear found itself during World War II. At that time Kingswear
had a population of about 800 who could buy virtually anything from candles to
haircuts in the village from its many shops. The population is now about 600
but the shops have dwindled to a very valuable village general store, the 'centre
of the universe' Post Office and a seasonal teddy bear shop. The number of
pubs has not changed since the war years!

There are any number of books and stories written about World War II. It is not
my intention to compete in any way with these other publications; although I
have included some background information where I hope it helps to paint a
clearer picture. My intention is, however, to offer a very local flavour of the
events of a small Devon village between the years of 1939 to 1945.

To try to achieve this I have made reference to a large number and array of
resources which are listed at the end of each chapter. The Kingswear
Historians' archives are full of treasures; the original Air Raid Precaution diaries,
Parish Council minutes and Women's Institute record books are all full of
fascinating detail of local life at that time. The internet, of course, liberates a
colossal amount of information.

Undoubtedly the most amazing part of my research was the time consuming,
yet fascinating, procedure of interviews that gave me such a great deal of fun
and information and fleshed out so many bones. This wonderful resource of
personal recollections will eventually be lost unless it is recorded now.

Hence talking to 'the locals' was a greatly rewarding and enormous privilege; to
hear some of their very personal, often amusing but occasionally distressing
stories from seventy or so years ago was extremely moving. To witness an
eighty-something year old man weeping as he willingly divulged a story that he
had never told before, left a considerable impression on me. The whole process
of talking to the locals has provided me with an enormous selection of personal
tales, many of which have never seen print before. The locals deserve a
considerable amount of my appreciation. I am also aware that there will be
others who I have not contacted or not been able to contact and who would
have been able to add to this story. I would be very happy to hear from anyone
in this position.

If I have misunderstood or misrepresented their tales, I apologise
wholeheartedly. I am well aware that memories and the passage of time can
influence dates and times and different people recollect events in different
ways. This may be an apparent cause of any discrepancy in the stories.

The first chapter introduces 'the locals', all of whom have a story to tell. Many of them lived their childhoods in Kingswear; some moved here during the war either willingly or by need. Some were in the Armed Forces based in Kingswear and some experienced the war elsewhere but subsequently became one of 'the locals'.

However before you meet the locals, I must offer my appreciation and thanks to the many people who have given help and information. Kingswear Historians has been the catalyst for me to attempt this book, and my wife Carolyn has diligently read, checked and altered my efforts. I would also like to thank Mike Goodearl for his expertise in editing the wonderful maps. I have tried to include sources at the end of each chapter, but apologise if any have been inadvertently left out.

I must also thank a number of people, as well as Councillor Jonathan Hawkins through his offices at Devon County Council, who have generously offered sponsorship to help get this story into print on behalf of Kingswear Historians, and to those who have helped our cash flow by pre-ordering books.

David Williams
Kingston
Kingswear
2011

The chapters

1. The Locals

The locals are the cornerstone of this story and have all been very willing and co-operative when I have approached them to discuss their wartime reminiscences at interview. Many of them have tolerated this on numerous occasions!

Reg Little was born in Wantage in 1927 and moved to Kingswear as a very young lad. He has lived here since then and went to Kingswear School age 5 before going on to Dartmouth Boy's School. He has a wealth of stories, photographs and documents, some of which he has already published. His 'Growing up in wartime Kingswear' is lodged in the Devon Library and is accessible via the internet.

Sheila Little was born just across the River Dart in Dittisham to parents who ran The Red Lion Inn. She went to the County School in Totnes until 1945 which is now King Edward VI Community School, 'KEVICS', before coming to Kingswear in 1940. Reg and Sheila still live in Kingswear and remain very much part of village life.

Frank Little.
Frank, Reg's elder brother, is often known as Jack and was born in Trowbridge Wiltshire in 1924.
Frank's father worked for the Great Western Railway as a bus driver after World War I. At that time GWR had their own bus fleet known as GWR Buses. This branch of the company was sold in 1928 to the National Bus Co and Mr Little was transferred to Dartmouth. Jack left school at the age of 14; he worked at the Noss shipyard from 1938-1960 as a wood machinist. He subsequently worked for Staverton Builders then started Orchard Joinery on Higher Contour Road on Mr Powlesland's land. The Westerland flats, where he and Ros now live, were built

on that land taken by Compulsory Purchase Order for housing. Jack and Reg had a brother George Herbert, 'Bert', who was born in 1925. He was killed in the Noss bombing.

Ros Little. Rosamund Bell was born in Brixham but moved to Kingswear as a one month old infant! Her parents lived in Church Park on Brixham Road. Her mother died when Ros was just 12; she then went to live with Mrs Parnell, who she referred to as 'aunty', at Agra Villas with her daughter and niece. Mrs Parnell had commandos billeted with her for part of the war, as did Mrs Pollard next door. Ros left Kingswear School when she was 11 to go to Dartmouth Girls School where she continued her education until she was 14. There then followed a period of working in the Co-op shop in Kingswear, before Ros transferred to the Co-op in Dartmouth.

Jack and Ros were married on 20 September 1947.

Edna Knapman was born in Lambeth, but then moved to Camberwell, before  being evacuated to Kingswear in 1940 at the age of 8. She came down to Devon with her siblings; 3 boys (Johnny aged 12, Derek 6 and David 4), and two sisters, the youngest aged 2. They all travelled on the train together, never having been on a train before, and never having seen the sea before. Although they all initially stayed together, later the three girls went to live with Mr & Mrs Bartlett at Mount Pleasant. He was a retired fisherman. The boys were taken to Berry Head Mansion in Brixham which was a boy's hostel at that time. It was a further 18 months before Edna's mother and 14 year old sister, Alice, moved from London to Brixham to allow the family to be reunited again. Edna was known as Lifebuoy at school in recognition of the soap her mother always used! Dad was eventually demobbed from the RAF to Brixham.

Margaret Fabian
Margaret Rowe was born in Exeter in 1934. Her father, Mr Rowe, was a flying test pilot based at Filton near Bristol. He stayed there for while but then moved to Hearn Bay. Latterly he was a test pilot for BOAC, the British Overseas Airways Corporation, and forerunner of British Airways. He died from tuberculosis in 1946 at the family home 3 Hillside Terrace, Kingswear.

Margaret remembers a lot of nearby bombing in the early war years. Filton, with its aeronautical industry and expertise, was a desirable target for German bombing raids. Margaret started school in Filton, and recalls many practices to get into the school air raid shelters as fast as possible in the event of a raid; the particular smell of the damp earth in the shelter still readily comes to her mind.

She was evacuated to Kingswear in 1940 with her mother and older sister, Mavis. They are seen here together at Hillside Terrace in 1945. She explains that 'the Bovey, Gunning and Westacott families were always here in Kingswear, so my cousins were always around' and 'I just remember having fun, with no sense of fear or terror.' She would often swim off Lighthouse Beach, as well as off Mill Bay but 'we knew where the land mines were!' They spent time skipping, and making stilts from string and tin cans, with also a rope swing dangling from trees over Higher Contour Road. On one occasion the rope broke and a lad fell into the road breaking his arm!

Nova Varney nee Bovey is Margaret Fabian's cousin. Although they have recently moved to Dorset, Nova and Peter have spent a large part of their married lives in Kingswear, and Nova was born in the village. She was also the recipient in 2004 of the Kingswear Award 'for work for the good of this community'. This is awarded and presented annually by the Parish Council to a resident of the village who they feel achieves that aspiration.

Gillian Bovey now lives in Brixham but she and her late husband Brian lived along Brixham Road in Kingswear for many years. Brian died after their move to Brixham. He was Nova Varney's brother and their father, Charlie Bovey, married Kathleen Parsons. Gillian shared with me many of the stories that Brian had told of his life and times in wartime Kingswear.

Dick Harris was born in March 1922, and died in January 2009. His father farmed at Higher Greenway and then moved to Hoodown Farm in 1936. This land is still farmed by the Harris family. Dick was based at Coleton Farm during the war and married Mary Thomas, daughter of the farm's tenants, in 1946. They then moved to Croftlands Farm.

Marjorie Reeves was brought up on Coleton Farm, daughter of Mr & Mrs Thomas who farmed the land on behalf of Mr Rupert D'Oyly Carte. She married Cpl Bernard Reeves who was one of the very early guards of the RAF Radar site. She still lives in Brixham where they set up home after the war. She has written an unpublished autobiography, which she generously loaned to me, and which gave a wonderful insight into her war time memories. Her sister, Mary, married Dick Harris.

Mike Short lives in Instow near Barnstaple. He was 6 at the outbreak of war, whilst Reg Little seemed to him, at 12, an adult! Mike joined the scouts, remembering Reg and his father even though Reg did not remember him!

In September 1939 he was living at 3 Jubilee Terrace with his grandmother Ruth Short and her twins Peter and Doreen. Peter worked in a local garage and Doreen worked in Kingswear Post Office. Ruth's older three daughters had already left home. Mike's mother, Edna, worked and lived away, Dora had married Sam Cooper and Cissie was married to Alfred Smerdon and lived in Cambourne.

Here is the Short family at 1 Church Park in the summer of 1941. The lady standing on the left is unknown. A young Mike is standing between Alfred Smerdon and Cissie with Peter Short and Doris Cooper on the right. Sitting in the middle are Ruth Short and Doreen Wills with Edna Short and Sam Cooper at the front.

Barry Westcott lives in Holland with his Dutch wife, but was born in Paignton and moved to Kingswear as a baby. His parents worked for Mr and Mrs Jones at The Grange. They lived in Grange Cottage. During term time he would walk from there to school, but at times the road was closed if the anti-aircraft guns were in action. This would involve a detour round Millbay Cove where there was a small minefield! As a young boy the forces, aircraft and warships must have been compellingly exciting. It seemed to take over from the three R's at school, a point not missed by Miss Hayward of Kingswear School whose remonstrations 'did not help very much'.

Tony Read now lives in Plympton. In 2008 he wrote 'my father was in the navy and we all lived in Plymouth. Every time he came home on leave it was usually to the remains of a house and a reduced family. Before he returned to his ship he had usually fixed us up with digs in some distant town, hoping that Hitler didn't find out. We lived in Falmouth, Ilfracombe, Launceston, Penryn and a few other places the names of which escape me. The last place, and the happiest place, was Kingswear, and my big bruvver Pete and myself settled in till the war ended.'

Elizabeth Hearn was born in Leeds; her father was born in Dartmouth and worked there as a Teacher. However, during the first part of World War 1 he was in the 7th Devon Regiment and stationed at Whitby. He then gained a Commission as a Colour Sergeant in the West Yorkshire Regiment. After the war he ran a removals business but took early retirement in 1946, bought The Redoubt and settled in Kingswear. They ran it as a guest house until they moved in 1950. Mr Hearn generously gave the money to purchase Waterhead Creek for the Kingswear community.

Initially Elizabeth and her mother came down here in July 1946 followed by her father and sister just before Christmas that year. Elizabeth recalls that The Redoubt had been occupied by the Royal Navy during that year and needed a fair amount of attention to bring it back to the state they wished. Higher Contour Cottage, where she now lives, was the gardener's cottage. She was in the Women's Land Army during the war.

Margaret Rickard nee Heal was born at home in Kingswear on 14 July 1922 – as she is quick to say 'free French day' and not inappropriate for Kingswear! Her delivery was assisted by the village midwife. She went to Kingswear School, leaving for Dartmouth Grammar School on the day that 'the excellent Mr Wedlake retired, he was great.'

Charlie Heal, her father, was born in Kingswear as was his father and grandfather. He ran the shop where the Post Office is now situated. Charlie's uncle shared the ferry business with Tom Casey – Heal & Casey.

Sadly Margaret's mother died at a young age in 1942 after suffering a massive stroke whilst making the family's Christmas puddings at home. Margaret has never made her own Christmas puds since then. Her funeral was on the day of the Hoodown Cottage bombings, and her grave is in Kingswear Cemetery. Margaret worked with the Post Office in Torquay, Dartmouth and Kingswear. She enjoyed the teleprinter course in Torquay. Messages would come via the telephone wires and be printed on paper strips which would then be pasted onto a telegram form for delivery by the several telegram boys based in Dartmouth. Sadly many of the incoming telegrams would be conveying bad news to local families. To send a telegram the message would be typed on a sort of typewriter keyboard before being sent. In her course she was required to become a touch typist and the keyboard would have a cover to hide the keys.

One Sunday morning she was working at the Dartmouth Post Office and just finishing the 9am to noon session. She had locked the safe when a man in naval uniform came into the Post Office with a sad story of having no money yet carrying a bank book. Concerned that she was alone in the Post Office with this stranger and that the safe was already locked, she declined to help him. Happily the man offered no threat and then left. However, she was surprised a while later to be summoned to Britannia Royal Naval College, to act as a witness at a Court Martial where the sailor was charged with stealing the bank book.

After Margaret Heal married George Rickard on 1 September 1945, they lived at Two Waters on Brixham Road before moving to Contour Heights. After the war they took over the family shop when her father, Charlie, retired as the village barber, but they continued to run it as a tobacconist and sweet shop.

Topline Broadhurst was a Motor Gun Boat Commander based in Kingswear, but now lives in St Marychurch in Torquay.

He was born in London in 1919, and his father hoped that he would eventually join his Lloyd's insurance business. However after a war spent outdoors, he could not tolerate the confines of London. Many family holidays had been spent in Devon, so a move south seemed logical. He farmed in Bishopsteignton, with a dairy herd as well as pigs, and acquired a passion for roses. He became part of many radio broadcasts on gardening, especially offering advice on roses.

Why the name Topline? When he had charge of his own boat, everything had to be just right, just so, in perfect condition – 'Topline'. When Radio Telegraphy came along everyone had to have their own call signs, so his became 'Topline.' He declines to reveal his real first name as it is 'too much of a mouthful'.

He went into the Royal Navy in 1940 as a seaman, and then was promoted to bosun on the cruiser HMS Nigeria. They had sailed from Scapa Flow down the Irish Sea and headed to Plymouth for repairs. While the ship was in dock, the crew took the opportunity to go to the cinema. That coincided with the first bombings of the city. Half way through the film, a message was displayed on the screen 'would all Royal Naval personnel return to their ships immediately'. They were able to leave Plymouth as fast as possible to see the city glowing behind them, but also aware they were silhouetted by the fires and potentially very vulnerable to attack. They then headed back towards Scapa Flow with orders to pursue the infamous German battleships Scharnhorst and Gneisnau, but missed them (with some relief, recalls Topline, in view of their awesome fire power).

Dennis Thyer lived in Cwmbran for 51 years. His family moved from Stoke Fleming to Kingswear in about 1940, and they lived at 3 College View in Fore Street. His father was a carpenter for the Philip shipyard at Sandquay. After the war when the work in the shipyards dwindled, they moved to Brixham. His father remained a gardener for the rest of his working life. Dennis grew up with Reg Little and remained a life long friend.

The Creek incident.

PLUCKY RESCUE.

Boy's Costume Caught by Nail on Raft.

KINGSWEAR CREEK INCIDENT.

On Sunday afternoon several boys were swimming in the Kingswear Creek, when one of them got into difficulties. Edward Hopper, aged 11½, son of Mr. Wilfred Hopper, or College View, Kingswear, and now serving in the Army, who is a strong swimmer, dived under a raft which had been made by local boys. Just as his head was emerging from the water, his bathing custume got caught on a nail protruding on the under side of the raft, and he was held fast. All his struggles to free himself were in vain, and his head was visible for an instant only at a time.

Terence Satchell, aged 11, and Alan Dudley, 12, who saw Hopper's struggles, thought at first he was gaining, but soon realised his peril. They dashed to his assistance, and were followed by Derek Thyer, aged 15 years, elder son of Mr. F. C. Thyer, of 3, College View.

Thyer eventually succeeded in extricating the boy. They got him safely into the mud in a very exhausted condition, where after a rest, he was able to proceed to his home. Had it not been for the presence of mind and pluck of Derek Thyer, it is most likely that Hopper would have been drowned. All the four boys are strong swimmers.

A group of boys aged 11-12 would swim in Kingswear Creek by the railway bridge on the Hoodown side.

There is a gravel beach there which dries out to mud but at half tide or higher offers 'a good swim.' These boys had made a raft out of an old door lashed to some 40 gallon drums. It was a nice day so the water was very tempting and the boys were swimming under the raft and out the other side, one boy in particular was doing it many times. Teddy 'Spud' Hopper was an evacuee from London, Dennis remembers, and on one occasion he did not surface after diving under the raft. The other lads felt he was fooling around. Dennis was also on the beach with trunks on ready to swim. He saw what was happening got into the water and dragged the raft closer to the beach so they could tip it up to release Spud. His trunks were caught on a nail. They dragged him onto the beach, gave him mouth-to-mouth resuscitation until he coughed and spluttered and recovered.

All this was being watched by a Naval sentry who was guarding the torpedo stores on the water's edge just the other side of the railway bridge. He informed the police who subsequently interviewed Dennis, aged 15, Alan Dudley, an evacuee with his twin brother, and Terry Satchell, a local lad, as well as the boys in the other group. It was following this that the three older boys were awarded the Royal Humane Society Certificate of Merit.

The Royal Humane Society was not the only organisation to feel that these lads deserved some recognition and praise. Dennis Thyer was a Patrol Leader and together with Terrence Satchell and Alan Dudley they received the Scouts' Certificate of Gallantry. Dennis died in 2009

Scouts' Gallantry.

CERTIFICATES FOR THREE KINGSWEAR BOYS.

The Scouts' Certificate of Gallantry has been awarded to Patrol Leader D. Thyer and Scouts Alan Dudley and Terrence Satchell, of the 1st Kingswear Group, in recognition of their gallantry in rescuing a boy who was trapped underneath an overturned raft in the sea at Waterhead Creek, Kingswear.

Four boys were bathing in the creek and playing with a raft. One of them, 11-years-old Edward Hopper, was on the raft when it overturned. His bathing costume became caught on a nail and he was held underneath.

The three Scouts, who were on the bank, immediately entered the water and swam to his assistance. Satchell, only 11 years old, was the first to arrive and, realising that he himself could not free the boy, held his head above water until his companions arrived. Together all the Scouts swam with the raft and the boy to shallow water, where they were able to free him and carry him ashore.

There was great danger of the boys becoming exhausted and of themselves becoming entangled in the raft, and there is no doubt that Hopper owes his life to the action of these three Scouts.

Terry Satchell was born on 9 November 1932 at the Belgrave Flats, his family later moved to Hillside Terrace in Kingswear.

His Grandfather worked with the cranes on Kingswear jetty, helping to load and unload from the boats tied up alongside, while his father, Francis, worked for the Great Western Railway as a goods checker. He never joined the forces as he had a long term ear problem. Meanwhile Terry's mother, also Frances, helped clean at many of the large houses in the village as well as helping at the station to clean the carriages. The carriage cleaners had their own hut by the signal box.

Terry's Certificate of Gallantry presented by The Boy Scouts Association.

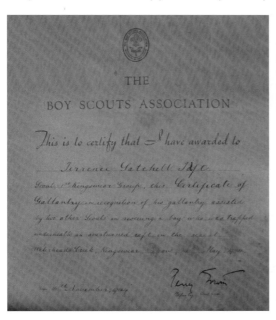

Terry joined the Post Office and eventually worked in Paignton where he and his wife lived in their retirement. Terry died in 2009.

Jack Eveleigh was born in Gittisham, near Honiton, in East Devon on 8 August 1922. The family moved to Kingswear in 1935 at about the time of the Silver Jubilee, his father was a gardener.

Jack left school at 14 and started to work for Mr Scoble, the butcher in Kingswear, but his father said that he should work for GWR instead. Certainly the pay was better, initially at 15/- per week. He enjoyed his work on the railway and continued to work as a signalman for the rest of his working life. He now lives in Brixham.

Jack's original intention was to join the Navy. Two episodes persuaded him to

join the RAF instead. On one occasion he was cycling by Hoodown when he saw a Heinkel 111 cruising at about 4000ft apparently on a reconnaissance trip. He was horrified that there was no response from any of the numerous vessels in the Dart until the plane was disappearing over the hill and a solitary shell was fired from the river.

The other occasion was when two RAF Westland Whirlwinds, seen below, came low down the river to receive a vigorous shelling from our own boats! Jack described them as very characteristic planes with a curious T shaped tail and distinctive note from their two Rolls Royce Pegasus engines. Both planes happily escaped unharmed but Jack thought that the Navy was not for him!

Once in the RAF he underwent training with some time spent in St John's Wood

in London, and even using Lord's Cricket Ground as a training site. Hardly cricket! He then established himself as a Lancaster air gunner involved in many raids over Germany before finding himself involved in food aid drops over devastated and desolate Holland at the end of the war.

Sylvia Payne moved to Kingswear in 1927 age 4 to live with her aunt at La Scala in Beacon Road. Her father had died shortly before that. Later she moved to Torquay with her mother before moving to Treby Farm in Yealmton in 1942 where, at the age of 19, she became a Land Girl for the rest of the war. She was mainly involved with cattle, feeding the calves and being sure to be up in time for the 5am milking. The afternoon milking was at 4pm. There were 25 milking cows, and it was all done by hand as the farm had no mechanisation at that time.

Betty Chapman was born in Paignton but now lives in Ipplepen. She was a Land Girl during the war and was initially based at Woodhuish Farm with Mr and Mrs Cannon together with another girl.

Betty in 2009 and in her wartime uniform.

Hilda Wallace was born on 17 May 1925 in Liverpool. She always wanted to live and work in the countryside so was delighted to have the opportunity to join the Women's Land Army and initially was placed at Halsanger Farm in Ashburton. However better still was a move to Kingston Farm with Mr and Mrs Coaker. She arrived there in late 1944 and stayed until the end of the war. Her bedroom was on the first floor and very comfortably furnished. Mr Coaker would use a bell system from downstairs for calling the rooms when it was time to get up. Mr Coaker had a fine herd of prizewinning Red Devon cattle which she helped to milk, by hand of course. Mr Coaker had a weary old Austin 16 car which Hilda would drive for milk delivery round the village. Mr Coaker taught Hilda to drive which she continued to do on a provisional licence as driving tests were not available at that time.

The housewives would leave a note on the doorstep asking for the amount of milk they needed, and perhaps leaving a suitable jug as well. Better still was the biscuits and tea she was routinely offered on her rounds. Mr Coaker later acquired a newer van to help in the deliveries. The Coaker's latterly had a dairy shop down towards the Lower Ferry. There was another Women's Land Army girl who worked with Hilda; called Ethel, who came from Manchester and stayed in 2 Kingston Farm Cottages with Mr and Mrs Gerry.

Hilda remembers Mr and Mrs Coaker as being elderly but very kind and a little posher than her working class Liverpool background. Mrs Coaker was organised and methodical, and Mr Coaker was a good businessman. Hilda was very happy during her stay at Kingston Farm. She now lives in Plymouth.

Maurice Ashton was born in Hemyock and moved to Kingswear in 1935 when he was 7.

Bob and Edith Ashton together with their family, Joyce, Iris and Maurice, lived in Britannia Cottage alongside the railway line adjacent to the Higher Ferry road. Bob was Crossing Keeper at Britannia Halt from then until his retirement at which time he moved to Dartmouth.

Maurice worked as an electrician with The Urban Electricity Supply Co in Dartmouth and was apprenticed alongside Reg Little. He continued working with South West Electricity Board until he retired. He now lives in Brixham.

Don Collinson has lived in Kingswear for more than 30 years after moving

from Manchester. He was one of the founder members of Kingswear Historians and is now their President. He has been passionate about our local history ever since he moved to Kingswear and has collected a vast amount of information, pictures and documents relating to our peninsula. He is author of *The Chronicles of Dartmouth* highlighting our history between 1854 and 1954 and is referred to on many occasions in the forthcoming chapters. He has also written books for Kingswear Historians entitled *The Dart Estuary Lights, Marks & Lighthouses* and *Shipwrecks and Disasters on the River Dart.*
In 2010 he received the Kingswear Award 'for work for the good of this community'.

Pat Henshall still lives in the same house in Wood Lane where she was born in 1926. Her father, Sidney Hall was a plumber and ironmonger with a thriving business in Kingswear. He was also a Special Constable during the war working with the Americans.
Pat initially went to Kingswear School and then onto Dartmouth. Her father was required to pay for this. After leaving school she worked at Boots in Dartmouth, although for a time helped her father in his ironmongery shop.

Pat married Eric Henshall in 1943. He was a Londoner who was stationed with the RAF Regiment in Kingswear. He helped man one of the Bofors guns placed by the slipway at Hoodown.

Edith Mum & Pat Hall on Torquay seafront followed by 3 GIs!

Having been introduced to 'the locals', who for the most part were teenagers or younger during the war, it will help to set the scene of wartime Kingswear by mentioning some of the more senior members of village life at that time. Their names inevitably crop up in stories and articles throughout the rest of the book. They appear below in no particular order.

Mrs Frances Fenner was President of the Women's Institute throughout the war. She lived in Bryndart on Church Hill and was described as 'a very nice and sociable lady'. She was a regular church attender.

Mr and Mrs Jeremiah Melville lived at Kingswear Lodge on Beacon Road. He worked as the Housing Manager at Totnes Rural District Council, and had been seen collecting rents around the village. He served on the Parish Council and was a Sergeant in the Special Constables.

Mrs Melville was also on the Women's Institute Committee and the WI often met at Kingswear Lodge. She was described as a very efficient and capable businesswoman who was on the Rural District Council. She was also involved in the Women's Voluntary Service who would have converted the village hall into a hospital and have provided a kitchen in the event of the village being bombed. As a nurse herself she was involved in the Kingswear Red Cross Nurses who would have helped the Women's Voluntary Service in the hall.

Mr Lionel Fairweather owned the garage opposite the school and lived at River View adjacent to the garage. He was Chairman of Kingswear Parish Council until 1944 when he resigned to join the RAF, and involved in the Civil Defences. His brother, Jim, worked as a bank clerk and lived next door.

Mr Turner was an accountant who had an office on the South Embankment in Dartmouth. He was Vice Chairman of Kingswear Parish Council and lived at Wing Tor on Higher Contour Road.

Dr Herbert and Mrs Grace Hope-Gill lived at Kingswear House opposite the Trust Rooms on Church Hill. She was Vice President of Women's Institute and was 'a very nice but forthright lady' according to Sheila Little 'and typical of a retired doctor's wife with white hair'. She was very helpful in the village. He appears in Kingswear Directory as Surgeon-Captain Hope-Gill but was retired. He was, however, available as a doctor to the Civil Defence if the need arose.

Mr James Tribble was one of Kingswear's builders, who had a black storage hut at the head of Waterhead Creek, before the land fill produced Jubilee Park. James lived in Spittis Park and was Clerk to Kingswear Parish Council at the beginning of the war. His brother was also a builder and would help with government projects such as piling in the river and building pill boxes; the one built on Man Sands fell into the sea in the 1950s.

2. Shops and Businesses

After meeting the locals, a guided tour of the village will help to paint a clearer picture of Kingswear at that time. If you had walked from the top of Lower Contour Road down to The Square in the late 1930s, you would have discovered a community blessed with a large range of shops and businesses. Many of the locals describe a village almost totally self-contained; perhaps having a bank as well would have helped to complete the picture.

You could, of course, have caught the bus from Brixham as it made its way down Slappers Hill, past the turn to Kingston and Nethway, skirting the cemetery on your left and into Kingswear. The bus would turn round in The Square using the space in front of the archway by

The Royal Dart Hotel to execute a three point turn, or probably more like a six point turn! This photo is probably just post-war.

Margaret Fabian reminded me that Higher Contour Road has always had that name, but Lower Contour Road was called Middle Contour Road, and what we now know as Brixham Road was Lower Contour Road!

Near the top of Lower Contour Road was Higher Garage. Harold Lang was in charge here. Mike Short recalls that his uncle Peter Short worked at Higher Garage, owned by Couch & Stoneman of Dartmouth. The garage was situated where the Above Decks apartments are now. People took their accumulators to the garage so that they could be charged up to run their wirelesses. The garage had a three-wheeled van which was used to collect and return the accumulators to the farms in the area. The garage also sold petrol. Peter was responsible for this service before he was called up to the armed forces. Mike would often go with him to help. He found this quite scary as he could see the road through the floor of the van! Electricity came to Kingswear before the war, offering a free service with three lights and one socket, but not everyone took up the offer. Mike recalls Mrs Pippin at 6 Jubilee Terrace who was quite definite that she was not having that stuff in her house!

Further down on the right, and now Chris Hoyle's marine engine workshop, was another garage. This was owned by Lionel Fairweather. He was Chairman of Kingswear Parish Council until 1944 when he joined the RAF.

Jack Matthews was the village blacksmith, working from The Smithy, in, believe it or not, Smithy Lane. The building is now known as The Old Smithy at the bottom of what is now known as Wood Lane. He would not only make the horseshoes but he shoed the local horses as well. Marjorie Reeves, who spent many of her younger years at Coleton Farm, remembers her Uncle Jack. Her father's farm was largely dependant on horse power so fairly frequently it was necessary for the horses to be taken down from the farm for their pedicure. Jack Matthews also made hoops for children to play with; Reg Little remembers this well and still has the last one Jack made for him.

Hawkes general store was to be found in Ashleigh House, just below the Smithy. The Hawkes family lived above the shop and delivery of their supplies round the village would be by traditional bike with a wicker basket on the front just like 'Open all Hours.'

Next down on the left was the Dairy, on the site where the Kingswear Village Store is now. It was run by Mr Casey, the son of Tom Casey the famous ferryman. Jack Little helped Mr Casey with milk deliveries. Next on the left was the Co-op shop where Zannes Restaurant is situated. Jack Bissett ran the Co-op shop where you could buy almost anything from paraffin to 1d wreckers – a sort of small tooth-challenging rock cake. Terry Satchell's memory of Mr Bissett was to see him in a small alcove in the back corner of the shop shaving!

Next down the road was Mr Scoble the butcher. Terry did some work for Mr Scoble. On a traditional butcher's bike with wicker basket at the front, he would set off to deliver meat orders. Heading for Kingswear Court he went straight over the handlebars on a slippery patch of gravel. He skinned the palms of his hands and the meat went sprawling. However the meat was just about saved by the copious brown paper and string surrounding it but his poor hands were sore for some days! The customers were satisfied, or perhaps just oblivious to the events!

Mrs De Lisle Soady was a haberdasher who always had a good stock. Where you now find Charles Head's office, was a Sunday paper shop run by Bill Kelland. He also ran the station newsagent stall during week. The Kelland family lived just below The Steam Packet Inn. Further down the road was Mr Hunt's shoe and clothes shop situated just above Kingswear Village Hall, while

opposite the archway of The Royal Dart Hotel was Mrs Taylor's sweet shop. The Lower Ferry office now occupies Mr Stanleick's bakery. Here are Margaret Dart with Maureen Stanleick and Margaret Rowe outside the bakery in 1945. Mr Pepperall, the grocer, worked where the Teddy Bear shop now resides.

Mr Heal, shopkeeper, barber and postman had his shop where the current Post Office is situated. Home for Margaret Heal was above the family shop at 3 The Square. Her parents, Mr & Mrs Charlie Heal, already had a son, Louis, 9 years older than Margaret, and a sister 14 years older, when she was born in 1922.

Margaret's father's shop sold tobacco and sweets; he is seen here outside his

Charlie Heal
outside his shop
in The Square

shop. He was also the village barber and postman. As such he would also act as telegram messenger for the Post Office next door, which was owned and run by Mr & Mrs Wellington. Mr Heal had no car or bike so all telegram deliveries were made on foot. Hair cuts were only available after the post had been delivered, and might well be interrupted if an urgent telegram came through!

On one occasion just before Christmas there was a telegram to be delivered to the D'Oyly Cartes at Coleton Fishacre, so Charlie Heal set forth on his errand. The D'Oyly Cartes were well known as kind people, and when Charlie arrived they offered him a seasonal drink....then another.... and another. Charlie eventually arrived back home less than totally sober but full of good cheer! Mr and Mrs Wellington were staunch Methodists and thoroughly disapproving of alcohol. Charlie was not asked to deliver telegrams thereafter!

Margaret Heal is seen here with her mother outside their shop, still recognisable as today's Post Office.

Margaret recalls that almost everything could be bought in Kingswear, which was 'a wonderful community', although the nearest bank was in Dartmouth where the Friday pannier market was held. This was a frequent reason for a trip over the river.

Bill Taylor ran the coal yard which was situated at the top of Upper Wood Lane.

The Royal Dart Hotel was requisitioned by the Royal Navy and became HMS Cicala. The ground floor remained as a pub, but upstairs became the Headquarters for the Coastal Forces, who reported to Britannia Royal Naval College, with the top floor taken up as sleeping accommodation. This proved insufficient so Topline Broadhurst informed Col Hine-Haycock at Kittery Court that his home was to be taken over as well!

The Laundry was situated at the far end of Waterhead creek. It was run by Mr Mitchelmore who had a contract to launder the Naval College bedding and clothing. The whole process depended on a secure water supply. This came from the stream babbling down the valley adjacent to Slappers Hill and into a holding tank above and behind the laundry.

The huge increase in militia and boats that the war brought with it also brought the need for more facilities. Mr Mitchelmore was approached by the Americans, Jack Eveleigh reflects, to help with their laundry. He contemplated this but then had to decline the extra work as the water supply was inadequate. 'No problem', the Americans said. 'We will build you a bigger reservoir.' So their bulldozers and diggers set to work. The area concerned was extremely boggy and first one machine then the other got stuck in the mud! Poor Mr Mitchelmore then had no water supply! This was all happening just before D-day when the Americans left overnight! Maurice Ashton recalls that eventually extra bore holes had to be sunk to try to improve the water supply to meet the increased demand.

Both Reg Little and Jack Eveleigh recall that the laundry was staffed, amongst others, by a number of girls from Dartmouth. They would arrive by the 0730 ferry from Dartmouth and be seen and heard walking and whistling their way to work along the creek.

Reg Little recalls that the laundry, although owned by Mr Mitchelmore, was managed by the Bell family, his sister-in-law Rosamund's grandparents. They lived in a house between No.1 Waterhead Cottages and the laundry. The power for the laundry at that time came from a steam engine, which had a high brick chimney. The water supply coming from a stream as described above, down from "Oversteps" to the cemetery. This had originally been the leat to the water mill. A large square reservoir was dredged out halfway up Waterhead brake with overshoots and overflows to control the water level. Incidentally, the same pool below the cemetery also supplied the water for the railway station. This was via a pipe along the creek to a water tower, which stood alongside the railway cattle pens. This also supplied the railway engines near the turntable. All the machinery in the laundry was driven by overhead shafts and pulleys, which ran the washing machines and spin dryers. During his childhood he remembered the brick chimney being demolished and replaced with a tubular steel chimney during one of the college holidays.

'Every morning at about 7am,' Reg recalls, 'some twenty five ladies, young and old, came across the ferry, passing the carriage cleaners at work, who had started at 4.30am, and much banter would ensue. The girls would sometimes sing as they went along the road. When they arrived at the laundry, everything was ready for them to commence work as the Quant brothers - Harry and Jack - had caught the first ferry and been at work for an hour and a half already. The girls would work until 6pm and even later if it was a very busy time. We could almost tell which day of the week it was by the colour of the creek!'

Mondays very soapy,
Tuesdays a little clearer,
Wednesdays blue rinse
until it was clear by the end of the week!

Cyril Bell, the son of the family who had managed the laundry in the early 1900s, drove the lorry which collected all the dirty laundry. It contained baskets and bags. He visited the naval establishments at Plymouth and, during the war, the hotels in Paignton and Torquay, which had been taken over for officers' flight training. If he had any spare time he used to work in the laundry.

Reg continues 'tThe Royal Navy always used brown sugar. Cyril Bell used to collect the sacks on his rounds and returned them to the laundry. (Jamaica paid their taxes in rum and sugar in lieu of cash, we understood). Cyril and the Quant brothers used to shake out the sacks and share out the considerable amount of sugar which was left in them. Sugar was tightly rationed in the war. One day they were engaged in shaking the sacks and Mr Mitchelmore came in. They had to tell him what was in progress. Mr Mitchelmore said he wanted to be "in" on it. John Isaac was sent out to the garage to get a sack which was known to have been polluted by rats. They waited until Mr Mitchelmore came and shook it out in front of him. When he saw the rat droppings he was horrified. Cyril and the Quants said "It's quite alright, it's easy to pick the droppings out". They were delighted when he suddenly lost interest in sugar sharing!

Just before D Day, a batch of duffel coats was sent to the laundry for washing. Reg Little recorded 'that some of them were blood stained. These coats remained unclaimed in the laundry for several years as the ship they came from had been sent on other duties. In 1946 or thereabouts some of these duffel coats began to leak out into the village. They were all wool and would have been very expensive to buy. In the 1947 blizzard, some of the coats found their way to the Teacher Training College in Salisbury where my fiancée, Sheila, now my wife, was studying. They were dyed in various colours and were greatly appreciated in that very bad winter. Indeed, they are still remembered at the annual college reunions!'

Thanks to Jack & Ros Little, Reg and Sheila Little and Margaret Heal

3. The Women's Institute

At the outset of the First World War, the economic and social changes in the United Kingdom recognised the need for the Women's Institute. The men were off to the trenches in their thousands and women were suddenly needed in many areas previously thought to be totally inappropriate for the fairer sex.

The farming community began to realise the value of women particularly in producing and preserving food. Mrs. Madge Watt founded the first British Women's Institute under the auspices of the Agricultural Organisation Society. Committed to developing women's talents, the WI today has links with over eight million women in some sixty countries.

The National Federation of Women's Institutes was formed in 1917, and an executive committee elected, led by Lady Denman as National Chairman. Lady Denman held this post until 1946.

A regular monthly meeting of the Kingswear WI was held in the Wesleyan Chapel Schoolroom on 20 September 1939, the 14th year of the Kingswear group. The Village Hall had always been their venue, but the Air Raid Precautions had commandeered the Hall for their own use. Mrs Fenner was in the Chair. The minutes were read and signed and then the Treasurer gave her financial report. The WI record book goes on:

'As this was the first monthly meeting to take place under war conditions it was most encouraging to see how large a number of members attended. Mrs Hope-Gill brought a message from the Devon County Federation to remind members that the National Federation of Women's Institutes was an important national movement which had been founded in the Great War, and that the Institutes all over the country should have the greatest support and backing from all their members in these days of strain and stress. Nationally many programmes would have to be altered and curtailed but much local talent could be found and shared by the Institutes in different groups. We should have to learn to be self-supporting and not to expect much outside help in our programmes and members should remember that our friendly and cheerful meetings would go a long way to helping us through any grim days ahead. A discussion took place as to what special form of war work the Institute could undertake and it was agreed that surgical dressings under the War Hospital Supply Scheme would be attempted'.

Later in the same meeting *'Mrs Adam gave an excellent demonstration on the making of loose covers with many useful hints. She was thanked by Mrs Hope-Gill and seconded by Mrs Tabb'* It had also been possible to obtain 1 cwt of sugar for preserving purposes from the National Federation and interested members were required to give in their names. 35 members and 3 visitors were present at the meeting.

At the 18 October meeting a letter was read out from Lady Denman outlining the importance of WIs *'to maintain good health, strength and good spirits in the villages'.* Kingswear WI was now registered as *'a Surgical Dressing Working Party under the Central Hospital Supply Scheme. Patterns and materials would be sent later'*. Mrs Jessie Brown of Galmpton gave a helpful talk on Wartime cookery.

The Kingswear WI next met on 15 November to hear that the wound swab patterns had been sent but no material was yet available. The Treasurer stated that the bank balance was £5-3s-2d. Miss Burnell of Galmpton talked about first-aid and home nursing. The tea hostess was Mrs Tribble and Miss Blackborow was in charge of the Members Own Stall. The Annual Meeting was held on 6 December. The Treasurer reported a credit of £4-19s-0d for the year. 'Mrs Tabor gave a most interesting talk on Prague, showing a number of beautiful lantern slides'.

1940
The turnout for the New Year's Party in the Village Hall on 17 January 1940 was disappointing due to illness, abnormal weather conditions and ice-bound roads. However, despite the wartime restrictions, Mrs Weller and Mrs Tabb provided *'one of the best Party Teas ever given in the Institute'*. Members paid 6d for the tea and guests 9d. The Surgical Dressing Working Party was going to meet for the first time 31 January at 3pm.

On 21 February the members agreed to help collect waste paper, tins, scrap iron etc and the Secretary would write to Totnes Rural District Council for their guidance. Mrs Earle gave an interesting demonstration on rug making. Mrs Charles Sanders returned to the WI with her baby son who was presented with a spoon from the members.

The 17 April meeting coincided with the Kingswear WI 14th birthday. The Ministry of Food had *'allocated a certain amount of sugar for jam making in the summer of 1940'*. The following month a letter was read from the Chairman of Kingswear Parish Council asking that 2 members of the WI should join the Parish Council Salvage Committee to deal with the question of salvage in the village. 300 swabs had now been made.

At the June meeting it was agreed to send 2/- to the WI Ambulance Fund then *'a Cadbury's representative gave a demonstration on how to feed the family in wartime. Some delicious recipes were made and sold to members who were given a cup of cocoa at the end of the meeting'*.

The July meeting was held in the Methodist Schoolroom again and the President explained that this would remain the venue as the ARP would continue to use the village hall. The War Savings Group would start on Monday July 22 *'at Mrs. Northcote's house in Fore Street. Two members would be present from 2-4pm each week to receive contributions'*. Later *'the members enjoyed piano duets by Mr. and Mrs. Robert Dart, songs by Miss Hyde, and Shakespeare readings by Miss Ory'*.

By now the spectre of rationing was looming and at the September meeting a letter was read from the Totnes Food Office describing the particulars of free and cheap milk for mothers and children under five. By October a seed collection became available through the National Federation to encourage members to 'dig for victory'. At the December meeting it was agreed that the

New Year's party would be held for the Kingswear evacuees. To this end 17/- was raised.

1941

The Party was held in the Village Hall on 15 January 1941 with Mrs Fenner presiding. Tea and entertainment was provided for the Eltham evacuees and WI members. *'the hall was arranged with long tables and looked very festive with flowers and evergreens'* as well as *'crackers, jellies and blancmanges, iced cakes gave a most unwarlike appearance'.* The Rev Arrowsmith, vicar of St Marychurch, performed a conjuring show lasting an hour; Mrs Hope-Gill offering him a vote of thanks afterwards, followed by three cheers from the children and another three cheers to the WI.

By March the seed potato allocation had arrived and Mrs Scoble, wife of the butcher, *'kindly lent a boy to carry the heavy bags round to the members'.* The question of salvage in the village was raised again. *'The Institute had had to make a very strong representation to the Ministry of Supply owing to the neglect on the part of the Totnes Rural District Council to arrange for any collection of salvage from the village. Since the Institute letter had been written there had been a very satisfactory clearance of the paper dump'.*

Dartmouth and Kingswear War Weapons Week was held during the last week in May. During this time the WI Savings Group had taken £368 in Savings Certificates and Stamps. £2127 had already been raised for the purchase of Defence Bonds. Meanwhile Kingswear WI heard about the plans for a Dartmouth based jam making centre from Mrs Warren from the Dartmouth Townswomen's Guild. *'The chief item on the afternoon's programme was a spelling bee'.* The WI team played against a Dartmouth Townswomen's Guild team and *'the visitors won by 1 round largely due to the fact that two excellent spellers from Kingswear played on the Dartmouth team'*

The July meeting was held at The Mount, the home of Mrs Allen. The WI had arranged a Whist Drive to include members of the Forces stationed in the neighbourhood as well as guests of the WI members. Mrs Dart was in charge of the tea which was provided by members. 'Afterwards the Dartmouth Townswomen's Guild gave a display of Folk Dancing on the lawn, Miss Hyde and Mr Robert Dart acting as accompanists'.

The WI had been regularly supporting a girl in the care of Dr Barnado's and was able to send a donation of £1-10s-0d to help her. There was of course some red tape trying to get in the way!

MEMO. FROM

THE LADY-SUPERINTENDENT,
Home for Girls,
"Feltrim," Topsham Road,
Telephone No. : 3267. **EXETER**

16th July 194 1

To Mrs Tribble

White House Kingswear

Dear Mrs Tribble,

Thank you for £1.10.0 received yesterday for Kathleen Tooke. I will retain the money for the time being,as we are in a similar predicament concerning the clothes coupon question. Our children do not have ration books,so cannot buy for Kathleen. The question is under discussion with Board of Trade. I expect we shall be granted a general permit for Head Quarters to do the buying. I will return you the money or send it to Head Office just as you prefer.

Yours sincerely,

The last meeting before Christmas 1941 saw Galmpton WI and Kingswear WI challenge each other to a General Knowledge Test. *'Mr Hine-Haycock prepared and asked the questions and the result was a draw'.*

In her annual report, the President of Kingswear WI Mrs. Fenner, declared that *'during 1941 the Kingswear WI has endeavoured to carry on in a spirited way, and by its monthly meetings has tried to provide a relaxation from the strain of wartime anxiety which affects all its members. During 1942 we shall endeavour to continue, to the best of our ability, to maintain health, strength and good spirits in the village, until the day, which we trust will not be far ahead, when victory and peace shall come.'*

1942
Sir Harold Clayton spoke to the March meeting on 'The Dalmatian Coast in Italy in peace time' and *'showing many fascinating lantern slides'* and then in April the WI celebrated their 16th birthday with *'thanks to Mr Stanleick for being able to make such a delicious birthday cake in wartime.'*

In May the President announced that Mrs. Tabb was getting on well in the Dartmouth Hospital. A jar of calves' foot jelly and a cake had been sent to her from all the members with wishes for a speedy recovery. She also announced an outing on June 10 to pick foxglove leaves for medicinal purposes. One venue was *'the golf links by kind permission of Mr Roberts',* with *'a lovely picnic tea kindly provided by Mrs. Caunter. A number of WI members, together with 'the Girl Guides, collected nearly 1.5 cwt, and dispatched them to Newton Abbot.'*

The President announced in November that the WI War Savings group had *'won the distinction of having its name inscribed on a tank as a result of the Tanks for Attack Campaign.'*

1943

Early in 1943 saw two New Year's Parties in the Hall when *'the entertainment took the form of a social and members of HM Forces and representatives of Allied Nations were the guests'.* These events were an outstanding success with the WI being congratulated on the cheerful informal and friendly evenings, which included games, music and dancing. The singing of Auld Lang Syne and the National Anthem brought the evening to a close.

The members continued to support a child at one the Barnado's Homes, as they had done over a period of ten years. They now learnt from Mrs. Fenner that Kathleen Tooke would be leaving the home and that another little girl would be supported by the WI. The postal order of 15/- must have been very welcome, especially as it was equivalent to a modest weeks wages.

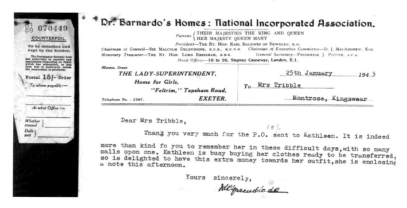

In April Kingswear WI celebrated its 17th birthday. Mrs. Fenner the President *'wished the institute very many happy returns'* and the Secretary then read the minutes of the very first meeting held on 21st 1926. Current members who had been at that initial meeting included Mrs. Fenner, Clifford, Tabb, Melville, Tribble, Edgecombe, Gunning, Thompson and Weller as well as Miss Blackborow. The meeting also sent a Greetings Telegram to HRH Princess Elizabeth on her 17th birthday. At the next meeting a letter was read from the Lady-in-Waiting to the Princess thanking members for their greetings. They were also being encouraged to become blood donors.

The June meeting was held in the garden of Ridley House, by kind permission of Mrs. Kyffin, with a talk on the Royal Navy given by Lt. Commander Mitchell. He gave *'a graphic description of the work of the Senior Service and special praise to the splendid work of the WRNS during the war'.*

Members travelled from Strete, Blackawton, Marldon, Galmpton, Stokenham, Berry Pomeroy and Thurlestone WIs to join the October meeting and were involved in *'a most amusing Brains Trust'.* A Bring-and-Buy sale was to be held in the Village Hall at the end of the month with an admission fee of 2d.

1944

The 1944 New Year's Parties were held on 19 and 20 January in the Hall. Once again members of HM Forces were invited together with the Vicar of Kingswear. The music was played by the Jupiter Dance Band. Mrs. Fenner as President *'welcomed the guests saying it gave the WI members great pleasure to entertain members of the forces, both men and women, and she told them that it was a small cost of appreciation to them for all their sacrifices they were making in this war'.* The cost of these parties was £1-1s-7d with most of the costs absorbed by individual members, and special thanks were given to the Refreshment Committee.

The Members were told at the next meeting that the annual subscription was to be raised to 2/6d, but that blow was softened by the *'most instructive demonstration on Wartime Cookery given by Miss Crocker of Dartmouth Urban Electric Light Co'.* The members had held their own cookery competition to make the best cheese dish and Miss Crocker was invited to be the judge. Mrs Jordain won the competition with Mrs. Hope-Gill coming second.

The Institute's 18th birthday party was held on 19 April 1944 with Women's Land Army, HM Forces, Student Nurses and the Vicar as guests. The supper was given by the members and 'cigarettes were given by Miss Head, Mrs. Turner and Mrs. Wilton'.

The present members *'who had joined the Kingswear WI at its foundation were given buttonholes of camellias, and as each member came up to collect her posy, was greeted with a round of applause'.* The party concluded with the singing of Auld Lang Syne and the National Anthem.

In July the Treasurer announced the contributions made by the Kingswear WI in the Dartmouth and Kingswear Salute the Soldiers Week. The Kingswear WI and Parish Savings Group had raised £3255-10-6, entertainments £52-1s-5d and raffles £40-7s-0d making an incredible total of £3347-18s-11d!

In September 34 members heard that the serious water shortage in Kingswear had been discussed at a special committee meeting which had *'agreed that letters should be written to the proper authorities with regard to the water supply'.* Answers came from the Admiralty, Totnes Rural District Council and the Ministry of Health. The members were *'glad to hear that steps had been taken by the Totnes RDC to put an emergency water scheme into operation'.* Totnes RDC came in for criticism again the following month when a letter was written *'drawing their attention to the most unsatisfactory state of refuse collection in Kingswear'.* However the WI was thanked by Kingswear Parish Council for their keen interest in parish affairs and their timely letter to the Admiralty regarding the water supply. It was *'undoubtedly a stimulus to the Council's demand for a better water supply in the village'.*

During that year there had been 92 members with 7 juniors and 24 new ladies joining during the year. Mrs Fenner, as President, was keen to emphasize the strength of the membership in her Annual Report. She also stated that *'despite the war, the Institute has had a happy and successful year, and members can look back with thankfulness that our meetings were able to be held so regularly* and with no incident from enemy action, although for many months those same meetings were held in this invasion port, with the preparations for a gigantic Armada continuing ceaselessly around us'. She also gave due praise to the 'Forces who were training so tirelessly in our midst before embarking on the assault of Europe'. That year the Kingswear WI Surgical Dressings Working Party had made 1228 surgical dressings, using the Methodist classroom as a base.

Mrs. Fenner concluded her impressive report by saying that she had outlined the deeds and activities of her WI. She went on; 'These are only the bare bones. It is the Institute's comradeship, friendship and goodwill which has clothed them and made them vital and important. It is also to these intangible possessions that our members have clung in times of disaster and good fortune and which we shall continue to treasure more highly than achievements in a world, which is just beginning to free itself from chaos, hate and destruction'.

1945
Mrs Fenner was chosen to continue as President for this year and the first function was the New Year Party with The Albany Dance Band and 'a delicious supper provided by the members.' During the supper Mrs Fenner formally welcomed the members and their guests including WRNS and WAAFs. Mr W H Philpotts replied on behalf of the guests by saying it was 'a heartwarming thought that, in spite of the present troubled and bitter world events and constant anxieties, people could meet at such a gathering and spend such a happy time together, full of friendliness and good friendship.'

Each meeting had a Social Half Hour, and in March Margaret Rowe 'entertained with a song and dance with Mrs Watson at the piano.' Does Margaret, now Mrs Fabian, still remember her party piece?

By June the WI was focusing its thoughts on bolstering the Kingswear Welcome Home Fund. A meeting was held at The Beacon, the home of Miss Baukert. Only at the end of this meeting was the weather kind enough to allow everyone out into 'the beautiful garden.' However various games were played including guess the flower from jumbled names, and bagatelle won by Miss Boon. The total raised was £30, with a further £17-18s-8d raised from a whist drive and Bring-and-Buy sale the following week.

The Women's Institute clearly provided a crucial forum for help and support in the community during the war, as well as an opportunity for relaxation, entertainment and fun for the members during those many stressful months.

Reference:
The History of the WI on www.women's-institute.co.uk
Kingswear WI Minute books

4. The Women's Land Army

Women also had another vital role to play in helping to keep the war machine running as smoothly as possible - **The Women's Land Army.** At their peak in 1943, the Land Girls numbered about 80,000.

'The Land Army fights in the fields. It is in the fields of Britain that the most critical battle of the war may well be fought and won.'
Lady Denman, 1939

Elizabeth Hearn was working in a solicitor's office in Leeds during the early part of the war. She knew she was going to have to contribute to the war effort at some point in time. The options were to find herself in a munitions factory in Leeds or join the Women's Land Army. The outdoors and fresh air was much more appealing so, in 1942 aged 17, she asked for a placement in Devon and got posted to Lincolnshire! The farm she joined as a Land Girl was in Holdingham near Sleaford, about 100 acres and mixed dairy and arable. She opted for the arable side (the dairy Land Girl had to milk her cows on Sundays!). Helping her were several German POWs who spoke very little English and she spoke no German. She does not remember any guards or restraints and no dissention, but felt that they really pulled their weight in the fields.

The crops were sugar beet, potatoes, mangolds as well as wheat and barley. They had a blue Fordson tractor which would pull the plough and take the beet by trailer to the processing plant. The horse would pull the rake or harrow. On one occasion the waggoner had failed to attach the rope harness correctly to the horse whilst Elizabeth was sitting on the two-wheeled rake. The harness came undone, the shafts stuck in the ground, the horse bolted and she was catapulted forwards! The discussion between the farmer and waggoner was probably fairly blue! Elizabeth escaped lightly and was back at work next day.

Badges of the Women's Land Army

Much of the harvesting was done by hand as combine harvesters were yet to reach this side of the Atlantic. The cut corn was gathered and tied by hand and arranged in stooks before the thresher arrived. The straw was then made up into a rick. She remembers the VE day celebratory rockets in the sky and one landing on a freshly made haystack burning it to the ground! In the summer they would work on the land until 10pm during 'double summer time'.

Elizabeth Hearn in WLA uniform

During her four years as a Land Girl she lived in digs locally, often with families with young children. Her food ration tokens would be handed to the landlady, and she never remembers going hungry or without. Weekends would offer social events in Sleaford where there were often dances, and a nice local church with an amiable blind vicar.

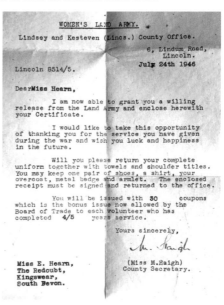

However, there was not much on which to spend her modest wages on. She believes that the landlady was paid as part of the deal of Elizabeth working on the land. The farmer paid her a welcome bonus on one occasion for all her hard work for him.

When she left the land in 1946 she received the above letter of release, addressed to her family home at The Redoubt in Kingswear. The 30 coupons were in addition to her clothing ration tokens even though she still had her shoes, brown shirt, brown serge overcoat and armbands.

As a Land Girl, Betty Chapman was initially based at Woodhuish Farm with Mr and Mrs Cannon, together with another girl. Here she would help with feeding the calves and chickens. The milking would be done by hand after she had brought the cattle in from the fields. Although the farm did not have a mechanised milking parlour, the farm was lucky enough to have one tractor and harvester. This helped a great deal with harvesting although the final stooking was still done by hand. The maximum use of daylight was ensured by harvesting until dusk. Betty would help Mrs Cannon take a full evening meal out to the fields to keep the workers on the go during this busy time! On one occasion a group of German planes flew low overhead on their way to bomb Plymouth. Betty recalls there was a mad scramble to get off the haystacks and seek cover as the planes roared past. There was a second land girl with Betty at this time and they shared a room in the farmhouse with their own beds and a view over the farmyard. This farm house, Betty remembers, was burnt down after the war and was later

rebuilt. Her stay at Woodhuish was fairly brief; she remembers that the food was not good and that the farmer and his wife not particularly kind. She then moved to Lustleigh Farm outside Bovey Tracey where she was much better fed and soon gained weight. She was married at the age of 19 and her husband was sent out to Basra in Iraq with the RAF, hence the badge on her right lapel. When he came back home she met him at Newton Abbot Railway station but he did not initially recognise her with her weight gain!

'We could do with thousands more like you..'

JOIN THE
WOMEN'S LAND ARMY

Hilda Wallace's experience as a Land Girl in the area was much more positive. She was brought up in Liverpool and had always yearned for the countryside. Her opportunity to 'sign up' as a Land Girl and move away from a bombed and battered home town had come. She got a placement in Devon, initially near Ashburton; but how does a teenage girl who has barely ever been away from home get from Liverpool to a small Devon town in travel restricted wartime?

Hilda takes up the story: 'A family lived across the road from us and the man worked in Birmingham. So it was arranged for me to leave with him; it must have been a Monday, because he came home for the weekends and returned on Monday. The first 'leg' of my journey was straight forward; I travelled with him to Birmingham. As time went by, I learned that very few trains went straight through on a long journey, as indeed today, one invariably has to change trains at some point. As I have said, travelling during the war was a nightmare. The trains were absolutely packed, mostly with servicemen and women; it seemed that everyone was in uniform of one kind or another. There were men stretched out in the corridors and anywhere there was space, asleep. One had to climb over them to find a place to stand. The chance of getting a seat was a 'pipe dream'. The trains were so crowded that men climbed in through the window of the carriage door, if they opened the door people would fall out.

We arrived in Birmingham and Mr Latimer found my next connection for me. In all, I had to change trains five times. The next change was Bristol, then Exeter, then Newton Abbot and finally Totnes. As you can imagine, by this time I was getting very tired, and was beginning to wonder if I was doing the right thing. It got dark early and I think it might have been raining, however when I finally reach Totnes it was about 8pm. This meant that I had been travelling all day. Totnes is a very small station and not many people got off the train, and they soon dispersed. I had no idea where to go to catch my last connection to Ashburton. The station was very dark because of the 'blackout'. The porter on the station quickly waved the train off; as it was obvious it was running late. I rushed over to the guard/porter and asked him the time of the train to Ashburton. As he rushed off, he said "eight o'clock in the morning", I ran after him dragging my case and said I had to get to Ashburton, "Is there a bus"? "No Bus", he shouted back and continued to rush off. At this point I was now the last person on a cold dark station, the tears weren't far away, chasing this porter, I asked him if he would ring Ashburton station as there was someone waiting for me there. He shouted, "NO! NO! they will have all gone home by now". (I must add here, that I was still in civilian clothes my uniform was at the farm. Maybe if I had been in uniform the guard would have been more helpful.)

So here I was, a seventeen and a half year old girl, miles away from home, on a dark cold station and the only other human being there, was the station porter, so I wasn't going to let him out of my sight. I continued to run after him and plead with him to ring Ashburton Station to see if Mr Herbert was still there. When this guy realised that he wasn't going to get rid of me, he agreed to ring Ashburton. Mr Herbert Whitley was still there, talking to whoever was on duty at Ashburton. So he sent a taxi for me. This whole day had been a steep learning curve for me, it was a case of being thrown in at the deep end, and I was on my own.

The taxi driver was an older man and he spoke very kindly to me. We seemed to have travelled quite a way when he, using his mirror said to me, "Where did ee say be gwain?", after fathoming out what he said, I answered, "Halshanger Farm". After a little thought he said, "I don't think anyone lives there". Well that was all I needed, I really didn't know what was going to happen. It all seemed to become a mystery. He added that the farm was very near to Dartmoor, he was shaking his head, still doubting whether anyone lived there. Maybe he was contemplating what he was going to do with me if there wasn't anyone there. At this point I didn't know who my boss was; all I knew was the name of the farm.

Eventually we arrived at what was 'Halshanger'; in the daylight I saw the sign on the gate. At first we saw a large house, all in darkness, no sign of life. The driver then noticed a lane at the side, so he decided to drive up it to see if there was life up there. We saw a large square building with an archway, which led into a courtyard. Remembering again that there was a blackout, and his headlights were shaded according to the rules, he drove under the arch into a centre yard. At first sight we saw the farm building, and then in the corner there was a house. At the sound of our arrival, a door opened and a man carrying a lantern came out to meet us. The big house we saw at the front was 'Halshanger Manor', the house, at the back, with signs of life was the farmhouse.

The driver got out and helped me out, obviously very relieved that he had found my destination, and I was ushered into the house. The couple who lived there was Tom and Annie Middleton and their two children. A boy aged five and a six month old little girl. I think the boy was called David, and the little girl was called Cynthia. I was certainly relieved that I had arrived at Halshanger, and even more pleased when Mrs Middleton said, "The other girl is upstairs", it wasn't long before I met Freda, she had travelled overnight from Manchester.

By the time I had taken my things to the room Freda and I shared, had something to eat, it was bedtime. I seem to remember that the next day we had off, to settle in and get to know each other. We had breakfast, and then went outside for the first glimpse of the countryside in the daylight. The first thing that hit me was the smell of the fresh air. The weather was fine and I shall never forget that first morning. The countryside was breathtaking, even though it was December, the trees were bare, but the grass was green. A short walk up the lane and we came to the edge of the moors, I was overwhelmed by what I saw; it was the first time I had ever seen such an expanse of real moorland. Nothing could have prepared me for this amazing countryside. All thoughts of homesickness had gone, at last I was able to live in the country, a joy I don't have words to describe.'

Having settled into a wonderful new environment, Hilda had to start work as a farm labourer. Because both girls came from the city, they guessed that this new life would be quite a challenge. 'Farming and country life was completely alien to us, and we both knew that it wasn't going to be easy' Hilda notes. The two men who worked on the farm found it amusing to have two teenage girls doing what was men's work.

'We did jobs like hoeing, haymaking and saving corn. But as city girls trying to be farmers, some quite amusing things happened to us. One has to remember here, that this was in the war, and it was 1940's, mechanisation was coming in slowly, we did have a tractor, but then the fuel was rationed, so we used the horses for bringing in the hay to feed the cows in the winter, and many other jobs. We had two big cart horses, they were both elderly, and they didn't want to do much work. We soon learned how to load up the cart with hay. The cart was a wain which meant it only had two wheels. One day I had loaded up the wain and was on my way back to the farm. The wain was being pulled by Tiger and he really was lazy. I had to keep giving him a 'smack' with a stick because he kept stopping. With the encouragement from the stick, he would plunge forward, and then slow down. This lunging forward then back somehow undid the chains from the harness at the back which were attached to the shafts of the cart, resulting in Tiger walking out of the shafts and heading for 'home'. Of course, the wain only having two wheels, the whole cart fell to the ground and much of the hay fell off. There was no sense in me rushing after the horse and bringing him back, because there was no way I could get him into the shafts and reconnect him. So, with my head down, knowing perfectly well what was going to be said back at the farm, I returned to the farm also, quite a way behind the horse. He knew his way home and entered the farm courtyard triumphantly. Everybody found it highly amusing, I can't remember exactly what was said, but it took me a long time to live it down.'

'The farm was mixed' Hilda recalls, 'so milking had to be done as well. This was done by hand, and for us to have to learn how to 'milk' was probably the most difficult. The men we worked with told us that we could say we were 'milkers' when we had two or three inches of froth on the milk in the bucket. Eventually we did reach this standard.'

My move to Kingswear was good; it was a completely new experience. I lived in the farmhouse with the elderly farmer and his wife. The farmer was called John Coaker, he was a dairy farmer and sold most of the milk himself, some in a shop he owned in the small town of Kingswear, and some was delivered to the customers. He had a herd of pedigree South Devons, all the milking was done by the men who worked there. There was one other land girl named Ethel and she was from Manchester. She lived in one of the cottages with one of the workmen and his family. We became good friends. Our job early in the morning was to bottle the cooled milk ready for delivery which I did with a van. I found the 'milk cooling' quite intriguing, to explain it isn't easy, the warm milk ran down the cooler, which was an upright, piece of rippled equipment, with a hollow interior which had cold water running through it. The cooled milk was collected in churns ready to go for bottling. Obviously the milk had to be cooled to extend its shelf life. The milk people received was not pasteurised as it is today; I am not sure if this raw milk would be allowed to be sold, as it was then. Mr Coaker taught me to drive in a big Austin Sixteen. I had a provisional licence but there was no test to take; these were suspended during the war. As soon as I could drive, I then drove the van, and my first job was to deliver milk to various people in, and around the village of Kingswear. I used to drive the big car also, but I should add, that Mrs Coaker would not ride in the car if I was driving, I suppose, because I didn't have to take a test, she wasn't sure of how safe a driver I was. I seem to remember that Mr Coaker sometimes got quite angry with her over this.

When delivering the milk, I got to know some of the customers, because I made quite an early start, some customers left out a drink and/ or a biscuit for me. After I had been there some months, Mr Coaker said he was going to the Totnes bull sale. He had a young bull he had reared on the farm and two weeks before the sale he had the bull 'ringed'. I was there for the ringing and it was an occasion I wouldn't want to witness again. I had wondered how this was done. The young animal was put into a 'house' and all available men were there holding a farm gate. The bull was ushered close to a wall and the men held it to the wall with the gate. Then the 'vet' or whoever was doing it, holding what looked like a pair of 'pliers' that one would use to make holes in leather, I wasn't close enough to see exactly how he did it, but it made a hole in the flesh between the nostrils, and I think the ring was inserted with the same instrument. The animal obviously struggled at what must have been very painful, and it took all the strength the men could muster to keep the bull from escaping. I can't remember all that happened after that, but I think the bull was kept in the 'house' until the day of the sale.

However when Mr Coaker spoke about the bull sale with his men, I piped up and asked if I could go as well. He said certainly not, whoever I take will have to lead the bull round the ring. Yes, you've guessed it; I said "I will lead the bull

round the ring". After the laughter had died down, I said very firmly that I would lead the bull round the ring. The boss said he would let me know. Well, I think after he had given it some thought, he decided that it might be a good idea to have a land girl to lead the bull; after all, it could denote that it was a good tempered bull. So he said I could go. I have to add that he also took one of the men in case I chickened out.

The day of the sale arrived, the large lorry came and after a difficult time they managed to get the animal into the lorry. To put it mildly, the young bull wasn't very happy. When we arrived at the sale ground in Totnes, the bull was charging the sides of the lorry and making a lot of noise. A policeman came over and ordered us not to let the

Hilda in 1943

- 38 -

animal out. I was beginning to have doubts about my bravado to lead this animal round the ring. However about an hour later; we had arrived with plenty of time to spare; the bull had quietened down, and the men decided it would be OK to get him out of the lorry. He had a halter on and a thin piece of rope through the ring in his nose, and I expect that nose was still quite tender. We had an allotted post to which we could tether the bull, which the men did. I was then instructed to brush him down, this I did for the rest of the time we had to spare. By the time we were ready to go to the ring he was almost docile. To end the story, I did lead him round the ring, to start with the bull was leading me, then one of the farmers said "get in front of him" this I did by holding him still while I got in front then everything was fine another of the farmers did shout, "How much for the girl", which was rather corny and nobody took any notice. The young bull was sold for a good price, and I felt very satisfied with my achievement.

I was at Kingston for about a year, during which time the war in Europe ended, and I decided to return home to Liverpool. I had only been home for a few months and I yearned to go back to Devon, to the work I had grown to love. I applied to return and I was sent to Dartington Hall.

After making contact through a WLA reunion held at Churston Grammar School in 2009, it was possible to arrange for Hilda to revisit Kingston. This was her first visit in 64 years! As she was concerned that she might not remember all the   narrow lanes that lead to the hamlet, she bought herself a satnav and drove from her home in Plymouth!

Hilda outside Kingston Farmhouse
64 years later

Ethel Forbes, the other land girl who was at the farm during Hilda's stay, lived in one of the cottages on the lane going down to the farm while Hilda was privileged enough to have a room in the farm house.

Hilda remembers that her first floor bedroom window, top left in the photograph, overlooked the lane at the front of the farm. The internal structure of the farm is largely unchanged but the use of some of the rooms has changed. Nevertheless after 64 years it still felt familiar. There was a bell system upstairs that has now gone. Mr Coaker would wake Hilda in the mornings by pulling on a bell cord downstairs which would ring the bell outside her bedroom.

The farmhouse seems to have changed little but now there is a wonderful panoramic view towards Start Bay that was not seen during the war. An aerial photo of about 1960 highlights this and clearly shows multiple barns and outbuildings that have been removed with the passage of time.

Hilda remembered the entrance porch and the front door. Mr Coaker had a desk in the corner of the room on the right, which is now used as a sitting room. He was described as elderly and Mr Coaker was thought to be nearing retirement. On one occasion, Ethel Forbes came to the front door and Hilda was there to open it for her.

Ethel asked 'is the old man in?'
He was indeed at his desk! 'Yes I'm here' came his reply!

Usually Hilda would come into the house by the back door, after she had been working in the fields or delivering milk. One curiosity was a hot tap outside the back door. Why would this be here thought Hilda? This was in fact used for washing the cow's udders before milking. Although there were a number of farm hands and the two land girls working with Mr Coaker, Mrs Coaker would do all the cooking, and feed everyone very well, and also be in charge of the house. She would however send the bed linen to a laundry. Although many of the barns to the west of the farm have now been demolished, the stone barn close to the farmhouse has survived. This was used as a cattle feed store upstairs and possibly housed calves downstairs. It has now been refurbished as a barn conversion.

Here Hilda reflects on the inside appearance of the barn before conversion in a pen and ink sketch displayed in the conversion.

It was not until late in 2007 that Her Majesty's Government officially recognised the considerable effort that the Women's Land Army put into the war effort. A ceremony was then held at Downing Street in July 2008 when a number of veterans of the Women's Land Army received their badges. The badge shows a gold wheat sheaf surrounded by pine branches and pine cones to indicate the work of both the Land Army and the Timber Corps. The Women's Timber Corps (WTC), also known as the 'Lumber Jills' worked in the forests to provide timber for the war effort by felling trees and sawing timber.

Elizabeth Hearn has now received her medal and certificate signed by Prime Minister Gordon Brown. The special badge commemorating the service of the Women's Land Army can be worn on Remembrance Sunday and other special occasions. With the outbreak of peace the WLA remained in existence doing vital jobs on the land until demobilisation was complete. The Women's Land Army was formally disbanded in 1950.

Reference:
Dept of Environment Food and Rural Affairs website
BBC History website

5. The Parish Council

So what did the Parish Council get up to during the period of 1939 – 1945? The responsibilities of the village Councillors covered quite a wide range of topics but they were mainly 'grave' issues as the general care and maintenance of the Cemetery fell onto their committee table.

Many agenda items would not be out of place 70 years later! A very large number of letters were sent by the Clerk to the Parish Council during this time, and many more letters to the Council were read out at the meetings. The majority of these have not survived but only their gist lingers in the minutes.

At the beginning of the hostilities the Council consisted of the Chairman, Mr Lionel Fairweather who lived at River View, Vice Chairman Mr Turner of Wing Tor on Higher Contour Road, and Councillors: Mr Taylor, Mr Melville of Kingswear Lodge, Mr Grant of Summerland Terrace, Mr Short of Windrush, Mr Chapman of The Beacon Cottage and Mr Harris. Inevitably there would be changes as the years go by, but at the end of the war the team has a very familiar feel to it. Mr Tribble was Clerk to the Parish Council in 1939, Mr J Armstrong taking over later.

Even before the war had started there was discussion about the suitability of Lower Contour Road as a bus route and the traffic congestion in the village. At that time only 28 cars were registered in Kingswear. A letter was written from the Parish Council to Devon County Council to ask them what steps they were proposing to take to ease this traffic situation. After the County Surveyor had made an inspection of Kingswear with the Police Superintendant they decided that 'a one-way traffic system was not practicable' and suggested a turning place at the junction of Lower Contour Road and Fore Street. Meanwhile the Highways Officer decided that it was 'not advisable to allow bus traffic on the road in question'

Tenders were received for collection of house refuse for the next twelve months from Mr Short, one of the local builders, at £52 and Mr Taylor, the coal merchant, at £50. It was recommended that Mr Taylor's tender be accepted. At that time the tip was on Mount Ridley Road where the current sports field is situated. The steps of the steep public footpath between Upper Wood Lane and Mount Ridley Road, 'the cardiac steps', run alongside the site of the old tip. Beware there is always broken glass here! After the refuse had been collected and any salvage taken, there would be a large bonfire on Wednesdays to burn the rest.

The Parish Council meetings which had been held every month up until September 1939 were changed to quarterly 'during the crisis'. One of the first points of discussion was about the cost of street lighting during the blackout. The Manager of the Electric Supply Co offered a concession of 10/7d (53p) for the month of September and this would equate to a reduction of £5-11s-0d for the rest of the year. The Council decided to write a letter to the Ministry of Transport asking for a ruling on street lighting charges during the blackout.

At the last meeting in 1939, a letter was read from the County Council regarding planned road improvements in Kingswear 'regretting the matter cannot be considered until after cessation of hostilities'. A further 5cwt of coal was agreed and ordered for the waiting room at the Cemetery.

1940

In 1940 the Council consisted of Mr Lionel Fairweather, the Chairman (seen here), together with Messrs Melville, Grant, Chapman, Taylor, Newton, Turner, Harris and Short. The letter regarding the electricity charges during the blackout that had been sent to the Ministry of Transport had been passed on to the Electricity Commissioners. Their reply stated that 'neither the Minister of Transport nor they had any jurisdiction to intervene' in electricity charges during the blackout and that this matter was 'only one aspect of a wider question of the effects of  war conditions on civil liabilities which is under close consideration by the Government.'

Mr Melville proposed that a precept of £120 for Cemetery expenses be issued whilst Mr Short proposed a precept of £75 for the lighting expenses. Both proposals were seconded and carried.

100 shrubs to enhance the Cemetery had been ordered from Dartington Hall and a cheque for 15/6d (77p) was paid to the Dartington Trustees, while Mr Short was paid 13/4d (66p) for the waiting room coal, and Mr Battershall received 4/- (20p) for digging an extra deep grave. Who for one wonders?

The statement of accounts showed a balance of £6-4s-7d on the general accounts, a balance of £11-13s-8d on the Cemetery accounts and a balance of

£90 on the lighting account. Mr Taylor's tender for house refuse collection for 1941 was accepted at £52. They also agreed to pay the Electric Supply Co £24-10s-0d less 10/7d for the quarter ending September 1939 and £10 for the next two quarters. This payment would include maintenance of the street lights. (Reg Little worked for the Electric Supply Company and one of his jobs, for a short period, was to keep the lampposts painted. The 1/6d he earned for this helped him start his National Savings Account!)

A special meeting was held on 7 May 1940 to discuss a letter from the District Council. They had allocated to Kingswear a trailer pump for fire fighting. This would require a crew of eight with four reserves and it was made clear that this arrangement was for wartime only and would not be used for any peacetime fire fighting. It was suggested at the Council meeting that the ARP volunteers be transferred to the Auxiliary Fire Service but then, after further discussion, the decision was made that a joint meeting be called to allow the ARP and Council to debate this.

A letter was also read from Mrs Melville, Chairman of the Women's Institute, about recycling in the village. It was accepted that recycling of paper, cardboard and metal was essential to the war effort and helped to conserve scarce raw materials. The District Council had evolved a scheme for this salvage and advised that a local committee be set up to discuss a method of collecting the waste, including scrap iron. Two WI members would be included in this committee.

There was another letter from the District Council suggesting that a committee also needed to be set up to spearhead the War Savings Group, and a member of the War Saving staff would be pleased to address a meeting. The Electric Supply Co had now offered to reduce the payments for electricity for the street lights to £4-5s-0d per quarter for the next three quarters.

The next meeting in June 1940 heard that the Chief Officer of Dartmouth Fire Brigade would instruct the crew, which had now been enrolled, for the fire pump. But who would arrange the pump's protection and maintenance? That would become the job of the ARP group until the end of the war.

Mr Tabb continued to act as Cemetery caretaker putting in about 15 days work every month and being paid £6-5s-0d for his work. Mr Battershall was still digging some extra deep graves and Mr Tribble, the builder, was acting as Parish Council Clerk. He was paid £7-10s-0d for the last six months work. He was also paid for supervising the construction of the new entrance to the cemetery including erection of the

new metal gates. These were made by Boulton and Paul. Was that the same engineering company that made the Defiant aircraft for the RAF? Did the new gates survive the campaign for reusing all available metal for the war effort?

Mr Harris of Hoodown Farm was asked to cut the cemetery grass 'and clear same away it being understood that no expenses would be incurred by the Council'. Presumably Mr Harris's stock appreciated this arrangement as well. It was also suggested 'that the meadow required cutting and this should be done as usual'. The cost for this was agreed as 17/7d (88p) and a man would be employed for a day to do it.

The Reverend Keyworth was paid £3-16s-0d as his burial fees for the last quarter, while the Revs Kirkham and Judd each were paid 4 shillings.

The Clerk to Dartmouth Harbour Commissioners wrote to the Council reminding them to put forward nominations for a representative on their Board. Mr A L Hine-Haycock was re-elected. Devon Education Committee was also asking for nominations for Governor to Dartmouth Grammar School. Mr Wedlake, who had been Headmaster of Kingswear School, must have been a very appropriate choice. It was also agreed that a notice be placed in the Dartmouth Chronicle to express gratitude to all the men and women of the village who were serving in the forces. The Council thought that it was inappropriate that the Council should pay for this, but agreed that the members would share the cost amongst themselves.

At the December 1940 meeting the caretaker reported that the roof of the Cemetery Lodge and Tool house needed attention and that part of the ceiling of the waiting room had fallen in. This was as a result of enemy action 'and the area would be inspected and repairs put in hand'.

The Minister of Health had written to the Council asking that a portion of the cemetery be put aside for burial of HM Forces killed in action. The committee agreed to this and defined an area that would be appropriate. In view of the fact that the overall space available was limited it was decided that 'the burial of non-parishioners be discontinued except by special permission'. The Ministry also pointed out that the Clerk to the Council would become responsible for issuing a Certificate of Disposal following death by war operation. A book of such certificates would be purchased.

Other regular payments were to Brixham Urban Council for Cemetery rates. These were £2-10s-3d a quarter. Frequent purchases of weed killer and carbolic amounted to £2-15s-0d. Three brooms were bought from J Palmer & Sons for 15/-The Council regularly considered applications for purchase of grave spaces. The December 1940 meeting approved purchases by Mr G Ash, Mr W Jolliffe and Mr Kirkham. The burial records suggest that there were no internments that month and the purchasers were doing a bit of planning ahead!

1941
On 21 January 1941 a public meeting was called in the Village Hall in response to the broadcast by Mr Herbert Morrison, the Home Secretary. He had outlined the question of raising fire watching squads in the community and this meeting was to consider such a group for the Parish of Kingswear. The Head Warden of Totnes was there to explain both fire fighting techniques to the fifty parishioners in attendance and the contents of some incendiary bombs.

The next meeting on 7 March 1941 heard that a deputation had been to Dartmouth Council to discuss concerns with the ferry. Although it is not clear what the concerns related to, it seems that there was a promise to 'go thoroughly into the matter and to inspect the plant regularly'. Perhaps some mechanical gremlins were affecting the service. The report continued that the 'float would cease running at 7pm, but a continued service by the small ferry from 6am to 10.30pm' was planned. Mr Tabb, the caretaker, ordered some more weed killer and carbolic and Palmer & Sons supplied a garden rake for 2/3d.

The Chairman presented a statement of accounts for the year 1940 showing a balance in the general account of £8-1s-11d, the burial account of £83-17s-5d and the lighting account of £108-7s-4d. The estimates for the next full year were discussed and proposed precepts of £30 for general expenses and £40 for burial accounts were carried. The large balance in the lighting account deemed a precept unnecessary. When the auditors reviewed the accounts during the following year, they suggested that £75 be returned to Totnes RDC from the lighting account. By way of comparison the Kingswear precept for 2009/10 was £12,000.

Mr Melville raised the question of the postal service. The Council agreed that 'something should be done to give a more efficient service' and a letter would go to the Head Postmaster in Torquay to ask for a second delivery.

In June, after Mr Lionel Fairweather was re-elected Chairman and Mr Turner as Vice Chairman, a reply was read out from the Head Postmaster in Torquay:
'In reply to your letter of 18 March I have to express regret that owing to exceptional conditions the delivery was considerably later than normal in certain parts of the village. I have taken steps which should effect a definite

improvement and it is hoped that you will not again have occasion to complain. I am sorry that under the prevailing conditions it is not possible to accede to your request for a second delivery.' Mr Short proposed that 'a letter be sent to the Head Postmaster expressing disappointment in his reply and press for a second delivery.' No further response from the Head Postmaster appears in the records.

Mr Turner had given a number of privet shrubs to thicken up the cemetery border and Mr Tabb complained that the Lodge cooking range was in a bad state of repair. The Clerk was to make an inspection and effect appropriate repairs.

A special meeting was held on 11 July to discuss a letter from the Kingswear Women's Institute regarding the position of salvage collection in the village and suggesting a new committee be formed with two of their members representing the WI. The arrangements with Totnes Rural District Council were not satisfactory, especially since Mr Hamilton had left. The meeting agreed that household paper collections should be made every Thursday and 'ask members of the WI to give all co-operation possible and to organise themselves so as to constantly keep in touch with the housewife in an endeavour to be sure that every scrap of waste is collected.'

The WI also wrote to the Parish Council about providing life saving equipment on Lighthouse beach. It was 'pointed out that the council had no jurisdiction over the beach only the right of way to it.'

'The Council in considering the letter mentioned that complaints had been made regarding the behaviour of users of the beach and they were rather inclined to favour the closure of the beach or place a notice warning users of the beach of complaints of misconduct, trespass and damage to property, also inserting a notice in the Chronicle for the benefit of Dartmouth users who arrive by boat, also to offer a reward of £2 to any person giving information that would lead to a conviction. It was also suggested that a letter be written to teachers asking for their co-operation.' This action was proposed, seconded and carried. The Lighthouse beach continues to provide plenty of discussion!

Mr Tabb applied for a portable washing boiler to be placed in the outhouse adjacent to the Cemetery Lodge, for a week's leave and for some white paint for 'the public steps.' These were all agreed as was a request that the agents of Mount Ridley and The Redoubt cut down the weeds in their gardens!

At the December meeting it was 'reported that Mr Tabb the caretaker had been away from duty owing to sickness and had rendered his account for 4 ½ days work at £1-17s-6d. After a discussion Mr Melville proposed and Mr Turner seconded that his wages be made up to £2-10s-0d.'

Mr Taylor continued to collect the household refuse but now wrote to ask to increase his charges by £1 per month 'having regard to the fact that the work had increased considerably during the past few years with the housing of evacuees and families sharing the same dwelling and the number of residencies taken over by the Services which frequently entail an extra round of collecting.'

It was agreed to pay an extra £4 to the end of March when new tenders would be invited.

Kingswear Burial Board.

By Virtue of the Powers conferred on **Burial Boards** constituted under the Act of Parliament, 16 & 17 **Victoria**, cap. 134. and the other Acts incorporated therewith, to grant exclusive Rights of Burial, **We**, the **Burial Board** for the Parish of KINGSWEAR, in the County of DEVON, in consideration of the sum of _____ **One** _____ Pounds, _____ **Six** _____ Shillings, and _____ Pence, to us paid by _Mrs G. Bradshaw_ **Do hereby Grant** unto the said _Mrs G. Bradshaw_ her heirs and successors, the exclusive Right of Burial in the Grave Space marked _1023_ in the _Consecrated_ portion of the Ground, at the Burial Ground, situate at KINGSWEAR aforesaid, being part of the Ground provided by the said Burial Board, **To Hold** the same to the said _Mrs G. Bradshaw_ her heirs and successors, for the purpose of Burial only, subject to the Regulations now in force, or which may hereafter be issued, with regard to Interments in the said Burial Ground, by the Minister of Health, or by the said Burial Board, or any other competent authority.

Given under our Hands, and the Seal of the said Burial Board, this _22_ day of _March_ One thousand, nine hundred and _Forty One_

The next item on the agenda in December 1941 opened discussion on attendance at the Council meetings by some members. It was noted that Mr Weeks had not attended since 1938; Mr Newton since June 1940 and Mr Harris had only attended twice in two years with the last attendance in September 1941. It was pointed out that this lack of attendance made it difficult to conduct business on occasions. It was agreed that those members who disqualified themselves by non-attendance should be replaced, and a notice served on them declaring their positions vacant.

1942
The Council decided in January 1942 that refuse collection should change from Tuesdays and Saturdays to Mondays and Fridays so that 'the man at the tip had greater opportunity to salvage items useful for war purposes' although waste paper collection would continue on Thursdays.

Mrs Dart had planted four shrubs alongside a grave without permission, the Council heard. It was proposed that a letter be written to her requesting removal of the shrubs.

Three nominations for the vacant posts were received and Mr James Fairweather, Mr Williams and Mr Dunn were elected en bloc. At the March meeting they were welcomed by the other members and signed the declaration of acceptance of Office.

Mrs Dart later wrote a letter of apology regarding her shrubs and for breaking any rules. She also asked permission for the shrubs to stay as long as she kept them well pruned. This was not acceptable to the Council. Mr Ash of London asked the Council if they could help with the upkeep of his mother's grave; they agreed to do this for 10/- a year, and also suggested that the iron railings along the north boundary be offered for salvage.

The owners of Ridley Gardens were asked to control the weeds on their land and the hedge at the east end of the cemetery should be topped off. Mr Wallace did this work and was paid £1-10s-0d for his efforts. No tenders had been received for house refuse collection but Totnes Rural District Council would take over but with only one collection each week.

By October Mr Tabb submitted a letter of resignation as caretaker of the cemetery. Discussion 'followed regarding the position of this action under war conditions'. Mr Turner agreed to see the Manager at the Labour Exchange on this point and it turned out that as Mr Tabb was over military age his offer could be accepted. His replacement would work for four days a week at the cemetery and for two days a week 'scavenging the roads to make the week complete'. The wages would be £3-5s-0d per week, paid fortnightly, with cottage and rates free. The Rural District Council would be responsible for the part of the wages for the two days of road cleaning. An advertisement for a caretaker and sexton would be placed in the Western Morning News and Herald Express three times with one insertion in the Western Guardian.

Thirteen applications were received and after some discussion a short list of three was achieved. In view of the travel restrictions and the possibility of difficulty of returning home the same day, Mr Clements of Higher Clovelly and Mr Balsdon of Beauworthy would be offered accommodation and their fares paid. Mr Bridge, the third candidate, lived at the coastguard cottages in Dartmouth and he was chosen for the post. Expenses paid to Mr Balsdon amounted to £1-7s-6d and £1-15s-0d to Mr Clements. The council agreed to an inspection of The Lodge and any repairs before Mr Bridge started work on 2 November. Two small scythes, a trimming hook, a short shovel, a broom, a bell hook, saw and draw hoe were ordered and the inside was to be papered and painted. Mr Bridge would be asked to help paint the outside of The Lodge; the paint was therefore obtained from Mitchelmores for £2-17s-9d and another 5cwt of coal ordered for the waiting room.

1943
A special meeting was held on Tuesday 12 January 1943 to discuss another resignation. This time it was Mr Tribble, the Clerk to the Parish Council, who felt it was time to move on. This meeting was chaired by Mr L Fairweather with Messrs Chapman, Grant, Williams, Dunn, Turner, J Fairweather, Melville and Taylor present. They accepted Mr Tribble's resignation 'with deepest regrets'.

Apparently two applications for the post had already arrived on Mr Lionel Fairweather's desk, but it was felt that a notice should also go on the Parish Notice Board with applications delivered to the Chairman by Saturday 16 January 1943, just four days after the meeting! What salary would this job attract? The £15 Mr Tribble had received was considered inadequate. Mr Turner proposed that it should start at £20 and rise to £26 after 12 months, and the applicants must be available during the day for duty. This proposal was carried.

de Gaulle and a Cross of Lorraine. These were to be kept with the parish archives and a suitable letter of reply sent to Lt While.

The Cross of Lorraine is part of the heraldic arms of Lorraine, which with Alsace, was annexed to Germany for much of the war. It was considered to be a symbol of French patriotism. The cross became the symbol of the Free French Forces.

Appropriately, there is a memorial to de Gaulle in the form of a 43 metre high Cross of Lorraine at his home village of Colombey-les-Deux-Églises in France.

A payment was then made to the Postmaster in Kingswear for £2-7s-8d for National Insurance Stamps for Mr Legge for October, November and December 1944. Although the cemetery was looking much better Mr Legge had 'over pruned some very fine shrubs, probably through inexperience.' The matter would be brought to his attention and Mr Chapman agreed to fund some replacement shrubs. Mr Townley of Alta Myra received a letter concerning the rubble left in the roadway outside his house, the Medical Officer of Health had written to his counterpart at Totnes Rural District Council and Mr Steele had agreed with Mr Pillar of Dartmouth that he would collect the house refuse. One other item was noted at that meeting; 'the sealed minutes of the Kingswear Invasion Committee were placed in the Parish archives.'

1945
At the beginning of 1945 Mr Melville was Chairman of the Council, Mrs Melville and Mrs Knott were joined by Messrs Chapman, Dunn, Hall, Newton and Taylor. Mr Turner had written a letter of resignation 'which was accepted with deepest regret.' Mr Melville said they had lost 'a very valuable servant and a charming chairman.'

They heard about letters from the County Council regarding road scavenging and further letters relating to refuse collection, this time from the County Medical Officer. Mr Townley of Alta Myra wrote again saying that the dustbins belonging to residents of Wood Lane Cottages were too close to his dining room window. This letter would be forwarded to the Sanitary Inspector.

Letters from E J West and G Byers were also read complaining about Miss Baukart's dogs. It was proposed that 'a letter be sent to Miss Baukert, calling her attention to the cause of the complaint, and trusting she would conform to laws of decency.' The Council also wrote to Totnes Rural District Council asking their advice. When it came next month their advice seemed very reasonable and 'suggested a friendly discussion with the person concerned.'

There was a flat in The Square, above Pepperels the grocer, which was vacant and it was the Council's responsibility to find a tenant. Applicants had to fill in an appropriate form, six of which were returned. Mr Melville, however, said that much renovation was required before a tenant could move in, and this was the responsibility of the Rural District Council. There was clearly a vigorous discussion concerning 'the full exposition of the Rural District Council's methods of preparing Pepperels Flat for habitation, and the maintaining of the council houses at Contour Heights in decent repair.' A letter was sent to the Clerk to the RDC complaining of the lack of necessary attention, and threatening involvement of the Medical Officer of Health if remedial measures were not taken. When Mr Bishop's reply was read to the Council 'some exception was taken to his attitude.' The letter is not included so we are deprived of learning more! However, Mr E H J Willing of Alta Vista in Kingswear was chosen as the next tenant.

Four days after this heated meeting came much more acceptable news; VE Day arrived at last on May 8 1945.

The next meeting felt more positive. The Rural District Council was now asking about the possibility of new houses being built; Mr Melville noted that tentative sites for twelve houses were found. The minutes do not name these plots. Some praise came from the Rural District Council 'thanking those concerned for the help given in the Salvage Campaign, and asking for their continuance as the need for salvage was by no means over.' How absolutely true, as even though the war was now over in Europe, rationing and austerity was set to continue for some years to come.

Thank you -
I am very grateful to Trevor Miles for copying the Parish Council records into a digital format, thus making this chapter much easier to bring together.
The Dartmouth & Kingswear Directory has been a helpful source of names and addresses

6. The Farms

In the midst of rural Devon, farming has always been a centrepiece of activity and employment. This use of our surroundings dates back to the earliest times and is still very much the case now. Of course mechanisation has changed the way farmers can work and modern fertilisers improve yields, but the cows and sheep are still there as are the variety of crops on which we all depend.

Dick Harris, seen here on 3rd December 1944 in Home Guard uniform, was a farmer through and through as was his father. Coleton Farm, Hoodown Farm and Croftlands Farm have all experienced the Harris touch, and the latter two still do. Dick reflected how the war had changed farming practices. An Agricultural Committee was formed with the regional headquarters based in Totnes. Local farmers acted as stewards to particular areas. Mr Coaker of Kingston Farm was the steward to the Kingswear peninsula. The Dartmouth and Kingswear Directory noted that Mr and Mrs Coaker lived in Kingston Farmhouse at the outbreak of World War II. They were tenants to the farm's owner Mrs Tivy. Mr Coaker was described as an energetic farmer who also had a fine herd of pedigree South Devon cattle that won several prizes.

Mr Coaker's task was to meet with the farmers and to advise them how to maximise the quantity of grain grown. This would include wheat, oats and barley. Potatoes were also subject to quotas. Mr Coaker would tell the farmer which crops should be grown in which field and which fields could be left for pasture. Dick Harris described the advice as 'compulsory but sensible'. Mr Coaker would return regularly to check that the farmer had complied with the advice. He was also in a position to loan machinery from local depots. The government paid for pasture land to be ploughed, so Mr Coaker's team ploughed many of the very steep and challenging fields leading down to Scabbacombe Bay. An unconfirmed story suggests that a Mr Cann of Woodhuish Farm and a Mr Hall of Lupton Farm were found to be cheating the government of subsidies during this time.

Mr and Mrs Coaker had no children and they are fondly remembered by Marjorie Reeves of Brixham. She was brought up on Coleton Farm from the early 1930s until after the war. Coleton Farmhouse occupied the site of the current barns of Coleton Barton Farm which was built about 1939/40. Dick Harris married Marjorie Reeves' sister, Mary, and farmed Croftlands Farm on Slappers Hill until his son, Paul, took charge.

Before the war, they would never work on the land on Sundays but went to church in Kingswear once or even twice. During and after the war, the pressure of growing as much in the way of vegetables and food as possible meant that Sundays became yet another working day. His fond memories of the Coaker's farm included that of two 'extremely nice' land girls, Monica and Ethel, recalled with a very definite twinkle in his eye and a chuckle. They worked with Mr Coaker on the farm. Mr Coaker was one of the relatively few car owners at this time. He had an Austin 16 which both he and Mrs Coaker would drive. During harvesting, with all hands working all the hours of daylight, Mrs Coaker would drive the Austin into the fields. The drop down boot would be bulging with wicker hampers of food to keep the harvesters sustained! Even Hilda, one of the land girls, was occasionally allowed to drive the car.

At about this time Mr and Mrs Jack Dowell and their daughter Cissie were living at 1 Kingston Farm Cottages. He was the horseman to Mr Coaker. He would look after up to eight horses and breed colts for sale. Dick Harris remembers him as 'a good horseman'. The farm was largely dependant on horses and Dick Harris reflected that most of the ploughing would be done by these animals. The first tractor they had was a blue Fordson in 1943.

John Hannaford was a farm hand who lived in one of the Kingston Farm Cottages in the early days of the war. He subsequently became a rear gunner in a Lancaster and claimed to shoot down two German planes. He, himself, was shot down but in due course married Cissie Dowell.

Meanwhile Mr Richard and Mrs Florence Rundle lived at 3 Kingston Farm Cottages and he worked as a farm labourer for Mr Coaker. They moved from Modbury in about 1927 and had thirteen children in all, although only 10 survived. Walter their eldest son became Head Gardener at Coleton Fishacre together with a time in the RAF during the war. Nora was born in 1907; she was in the wartime ATS. At the time of the Rundle's occupancy, the cottage was pretty much a two-up-two-down dwelling. Lighting was by oil lamps as there was no electricity in Kingston in the early 1940s. The spring water (some things don't change!) arrived at a tap outside the back door and would be gathered into buckets for use in the cottage. There were two steps to the right of the front door. Through a gate (the hinges are still present in the original wall) a path led up the side of the house and on the right was an earth pit latrine in a wooden hut. Torn up newspaper on string acted as loo paper. The latrine was pumped out by the farmer from time to time.

Mrs Rundle cooked on a cast iron range in the kitchen. However, she also had a primus stove on the bay window sill in the kitchen; Clifford Williams, her grandson who lives in Paignton, remembers his grandmother preparing 'the best of cooked breakfasts' on this single burner!

Richard and Florrie Rundle are seen in the above photograph at the front door of the cottage. This door opened directly into the living room; there was an oil lamp on the table and a tin bath would be placed in front of the fire on bath night!

The winding garden path led up the bank in the direction of Scabbacombe, with flowers on the left, and Richard Rundle's vegetables on the right. The second photograph shows Richard with Aunt Lil in front of the screen of trees making up the hedgerow; just two grand old pines remain from that collection.

Behind them the neat rows of plants can be seen and the photograph is of Richard tending his precious vegetables. Chickens were also very much part of the plot and essential to their self sufficiency.

Ploughing was time consuming. Two or three horses would make up a team which would pull one ploughshare and working all day would cover about an acre. Hard ground that had not been recently ploughed would need three horses. Modern tractors can pull 4-6 shares and cover eight or more acres each day. The inevitable attention of a blacksmith meant taking the horses down to Kingswear. Marjorie Reeves' uncle, Jack Matthews, was the 'smithy' at the bottom of Blacksmith's Lane although at that time it was colloquially referred to as Smithy Lane. We now know it as Wood Lane.

Dick Harris also recalled that Coleton Farm had at least six horses. Tom Percy was their 'excellent horseman' who would care for, feed and work with horses. Shoeing meant walking them down to the smithy in Blacksmiths Lane as well; perhaps this was a regular rendezvous for the farm workers. Two horses would be taken at a time; this tended to be a wet weather job when the horses were not going to be used on the fields. Jack Matthews the blacksmith was single and lived next to the smithy with a married couple.

The rabbit trapper and farm hand at Coleton was Mr Yeomans who would trap up to 3000 rabbits a year. The rabbits frequented the cliff top areas of the farm. Marjorie Reeves remembers helping Mr Yeomans put out the set traps at

05.30 and again in the evening. The dead rabbits would then be stacked in braces in wicker baskets and sent to Birmingham market by train. They fetched 4d per brace. More rabbits would be caught than could be sold, so many had to be buried in a deep pit on the farm.

Mr D'Oyly Carte owned Coleton Farm at that time. 'He was a Gentleman's  gentleman' and a kindly land owner who would ride round the farm on his horse. He thoroughly disliked rabbit traps. Mr Thomas, the tenant at that time, threatened to quit the farm if the rabbits were not controlled. Mr D'Oyly Carte decided to erect rabbit proof fencing all around his land along the cliff tops, no doubt at some considerable expense, but it seemed to solve the problem. He also gave Mr Thomas one year's rent free tenancy as a gesture of goodwill. Meanwhile Mrs Thomas would take in lodgers for bed and breakfast with some taking full board. Phyllis Rundle, daughter-in-law of Richard and Florrie, recalls Mr Thomas of Coleton Farm as being tall 'like a professor' whilst Mr D'Oyly Carte was shorter than his elegant, kindly dark haired wife.

Coleton Farm's cattleman was Bill Skinner. He would take feed out to the cattle in the fields by horse and cart during winter and was also an expert at calving. It was the case that on the farm 'everyone did everything'. Mr Thomas was an expert cattleman as well who liked to do most of the milking of his prize-winning cows, but Bill Skinner would help. There was no electricity in the milking parlour until 1953. Milking would be done before breakfast then the cattle would be put into the yard. After breakfast they would be taken out to the fields again. Most of the milk was collected from the farm in churns, but some milk would be taken to the house for scalding to make cream and butter. The milk was put into a pan in a bain-marie and warmed until the cream could be skimmed off to be used either as cream or churned into butter. This was for the consumption of the Thomas family and farm staff, but could be sold or used for bartering! There was a regular flow of tradesmen delivering to the farms. Fishmongers, bakers, haberdashers, ironmongers were amongst the callers. Many of these deliveries would be exchanged for milk, eggs, cream or butter. These tradesmen would also go to Coleton Fishacre house and to the chauffeur in charge of Mr D'Oyly Carte's Bentley and Daimler.

Also on the farm was a Mr Renier who had escaped from Alderney at the time of the German occupation. He arrived in Dartmouth with his wife, two girls and one boy with one suitcase! He was a skilled horticulturalist. Mr D'Oyly Carte allowed them to live in one of the Coleton Farm cottages as long as Mr Renier worked on the farm. Marjorie Reeves remembers that Mr D'Oyly Carte helped Mr Renier's son go through Dartmouth College. They stayed for many years on the farm but eventually went back to the Channel Islands at the end of the war.

Jack Eveleigh remembers Owen Job who farmed about 80 acres including Wilful Murder field and some adjacent land. He was also a part time signalman at the station and so a work colleague to Jack. He had a few sheep and cows as well as a good number of pigs. To feed these he would collect the 'pig swill' from the station with his horse and cart. Any food scraps from the railway dining cars was put into bins, often with non food debris such as broken glass and cans. This had to be sorted out before the pigs were fed and the debris was put aside in one of the barns at the top of Wilful Murder field. The pile got larger and larger, the rats multiplied and it became a problem to Owen who was unsure how to dispose of it. The bomb that dropped in that field provided his answer! Jack Eveleigh helped him barrow the debris into the bomb crater!

The pigs were slaughtered on site and again Jack would be around to help.

...el and Hilda in WLA uniform in Torquay 1944

When the deed was planned Mrs Eveleigh would give Jack a white enamel bucket with a cloth cover. At the end of the slaughtering the bucket was filled with the offal and other bits and bobs which Mrs Eveleigh would convert into hog's pudding and other delicacies. An extra supply of meat in a period of rationing was welcomed.

Hilda Wallace was a Land Girl who has written about her experiences at Kingston Farm during the last two years of the war describing her move to Kingswear as good; it was a completely new experience for her. She was at Kingston for about a year, during which time the war in Europe ended, and she decided to return home to Liverpool. She had only been home for a few months when she yearned to go back to Devon, to the work she had grown to love. She applied to return and was sent to Dartington Hall.'

Hilda on horseback

Amongst many other farm activities she discovered whilst at Kingston, Hilda learned to ride horses. She recounts more of her story in the chapter on the Women's Land Army.

7. The Defences

The risk of invasion must have been a real concern to the folks of Kingswear. With easy river access and convenient ferry slipways leading straight into the road network, what resistance could be offered?

If an invasion was actually threatened, the church bell would be rung continuously by the police. This would be the signal for action to the townsfolk.

Fore Street had removable concrete slabs in the roadway. These could be lifted up to allow explosives to be inserted underneath and detonated if needed, and so destroying the road. Pillboxes were built at Hoodown and Mansands which also had barbed wire defences as did Millbay beach. Jack Eveleigh recalls that there was also a cable lined with explosives running from the Hoodown pillbox across to the jetty to render the area unusable if needed.

It was thought that if any invading troops managed access onto the peninsula, they would face little resistance as far as Windy Corner at Churston. It was hoped that the narrow isthmus at this point would offer the greatest challenge to advancing troops. Hard luck on the folks on the rest of the peninsula who would be left to their own devices!

Air Raid Precautions (ARP) were proposed by the government but would be delivered by the local authorities. Their intention was to protect civilians from the danger of air-raids. In September 1935 Stanley Baldwin, who was then the Prime Minister, presented a document describing Air Raid Precautions which invited local authorities to consider plans for local protection in the event of a war. This would include the building of air raid shelters. By April 1937 the government had created an Air Raid Wardens' Service and during the following

year had recruited around 200,000 volunteers. These volunteers were known as Air Raid Precaution Wardens.

The main purpose of ARP Wardens was to make local patrols during the hours of blackout and to ensure that no light was visible. If light was spotted, the warden would alert the person responsible. The ARP Wardens would be responsible for coordinating the other emergency services, setting aside buildings for ARP use and publicising ARP measures to the local population. They would also report the extent of any local bomb damage; assess the need for the emergency services after an incident, for the handing out of gas masks and advice on air-raid shelters. There was even a special over-the-head gas mask device for babies. People were required to carry their masks with them at all times. Broadcasts were made to explain when and how to use the gas masks, and also advice that they should not be tested out in the gas oven or with car exhaust! Michael Stevens remembers that his first gas mask was shaped like the head of Mickey Mouse!

Local Defence Volunteers were enlisted; they were later renamed the Home Guard. The Home Guard's role was to defend the coastline and other strategic points, such as the railway, from imminent attack and invasion.

Reg Little's description of that time notes that 'during the invasion scare in 1940, the War Office set up a Defence Committee of about twenty two people, to take over control of the village if needed. At this time one of the River Dart paddle steamers was kept with steam up 24 hours a day in case the college had to be evacuated via the railway at Totnes in the event of Maypool Tunnel (the railway tunnel between Kingswear and Churston) being sabotaged. Roadblocks were put up as well as barricades by the higher and lower ferry slips. Tank traps were fitted across Bridge Road near the Higher Ferry, and about 75 yards above the level crossing, and by the village shop. These 'dragon's teeth' were concrete slabs placed every 2 ft across the road. They could be lifted and the

space underneath filled with explosives if required to demolish the road. When Fore Street was excavated in March 2009 to replace the water mains, the slabs became visible once more below the tarmac.

There were guns and searchlights at Dartmouth Castle and torpedo tubes were fitted at Kingswear Court. These were manned by Royal Marines. Mines were put in place across the mouth of the river. A boom was fitted across the harbour entrance from just above Dartmouth Castle to Brookhill rocks. The boom was

first made of timber baulks, about 10 feet long, 8 feet wide and 4 feet deep chained together. Reg Little said he and his mates would get out onto the boom and sit astride the floats catching fish! Afterwards they used steel tanks about the same size instead of wood - with sharp horns fitted! A steam boom defence

boat crewed by about 20 men was moored on the Dartmouth side. During day or night when a ship arrived the boom was opened by the boom defence boat. This is the only known image of the wartime boom.

The lighthouse and leading lights at Gomerock Point, Kingswear, and the light just below the Castle at Bayard's Cove, Dartmouth, were controlled from a tower at Kingswear Castle. From there a lead through the trees was fed to the lighthouse. This enabled it to be remotely controlled by the marines at night.

Paul Moynagh expands on the description of the risk of invasion by Germany after Dunkirk. 'Action was quickly taken to strengthen the defences of Dartmouth and protect the shipping in the harbour. This included the building in 1940 of a torpedo battery in Kingswear, at the edge of the sea immediately below Kingswear Court in Castle Road. It was built on top of an existing salt-water swimming pool and camouflaged to look like a thatched boat house.

Although the use of land-based torpedo batteries dates back to the 19th century, their use in the 20th century is virtually unknown and only two others apart from the Kingswear battery are believed to have been built in the Second World War. The battery would have been manned and operated by naval personnel but it has proved difficult so far to trace details in official records. Similarly, although it appears from remains of rail tracks that there were three launching positions, the type of torpedoes used and how they would have been supplied are not clear. It would have been linked to the overall defensive system for Dartmouth harbour including the boom across the river mouth, the gun position at Dartmouth Castle and the Brownstone Battery built in 1942.

It is said that one night the wrong code for the day had been sent by mistake to all the defensive positions. A Polish destroyer attempting to enter the harbour at night was seen and challenged by the battery. Luckily, in spite of the confusion of codes, the officer in charge onshore believed he recognised the outline of the ship and a quick call to headquarters confirmed he was correct. The remains of the battery are part of the legacy of the war years and it is hoped that continuing research will be able to fill some of the existing gaps concerning it.'

However in the event of a crisis, the Home Guard and Fire Service would be there to help....

in a raid -

Do not rush, take cover quietly, then others will do the same.

...as well as the Air Raid Precaution wardens with their characteristic helmets and whistles.

Mike Short recalls the ARP wardens coming to Kingswear School to show the children how to use a stirrup pump to put out a fire. They also had instruction on the use of the Morrison air raid shelter at the school. He and May Crisp were chosen by Miss Hayward as 'emergency children', no doubt a significant privilege in school days. If Miss Hayward knew of an impending event, she would shout 'EMERGENCY'. The children would then follow Mike and May down the school path to the air raid shelter. The ARP representatives also gave lectures in the Village Hall on the use of gas masks and how to act during either day or night raids.

Nova Varney explains that there was a Morrison air raid shelter in the sitting room of her family home Broadview on Higher Contour Road. This consisted of a table like structure with a metal top and wire cage sides. It was occasionally used for its intended purpose but would also be an excellent playpen-cum-wendy house and also as a table, although, because the wire sides prevented you from getting your legs underneath, it was not especially comfortable. This type of shelter was named after the Minister for Home Security, Mr Herbert Morrison. They were about 2 metres long, 1.2metres wide and 0.75metres high.

An alternative air raid shelter was the Anderson type introduced in 1939. It required a garden or outside space and was made of corrugated iron sheets bolted together and covered with earth to reduce bomb blast. They cost £5 each, although could be supplied free to the poor. They were about 2metres long and 1.5metres wide and tended to be damp and not particularly attractive places to try to sleep during a bombing raid.

Reg Little remembers that 'air raid shelters were built under the archway that gives access to the Priory, one in the road below the School and one on Ridley Hill opposite the steps to Hillside Terrace.

Following the invasion of Belgium, Sheila Little writes, about twenty of their trawlers arrived in the Dart and there was a dramatic increase in the number of wooden clogs floating in the water! For the Dunkirk evacuation only about eight agreed to go back to help pick up troops. The boats were taken away from the Belgians and given to the Poles, painted grey and fitted with guns. They then patrolled Start Bay. One is even supposed to have rammed and sunk a U-boat.

One of the Kingswear ARP log books survives and details many aspects of the organisation that was set up for the community. Air raid calls were logged giving the day and date as well as the time. Between 6 July 1940 and 10 March 1941, 260 such calls were received. The log also records the names of the first aid volunteers and wardens, and who received the 57 stirrup pumps from the

ARP and where they lived. At stocktaking on 17 March 1941 the equipment consisted of 13 steel helmets, 7 anti-gas suits, 7 rubber boots, 4 steel stretchers, 3 rattles, 5 whistles and a pot of anti-gas ointment amongst other items. There was a ladder register as well; 33 folks had a total of 57 ladders available around the village. The list noted 18 fire watchers. 24 cars and 3 vans were licensed in the village in March 1941 as well as two lorries owned by Mr Tribble the builder and Mr Hart. There was even a register of who had been given ARP helmets, Reg Little and Margaret Heal appear on the list – probably the youngest at the time.

The log book includes the following 17 point questionnaire for the Defence Committee to consider, with their answers to be given on the opposite page. The answer given is 'yes' unless a bracketed response appears after the question.

1. Have arrangements been made for the care and treatment of casualties when it becomes impossible to go outside the community area, including simple cleansing of persons contaminated by gas?
2. Do you know what private or voluntary medical supplies are available in your locality?
3. Are you aware of the emergency medical arrangements?
4. Has a survey of emergency water supplies been carried out, and the means of getting it and carrying it?
5. What plans have been made for emergency sanitation? (use of buckets)
6. What plans have been made for emergency shelter against bombing? (2 air raid shelters for public protection)
7. Is there full co-operation with the Food Executive Officer or Voluntary Food Officer and have they prepared for incidents of invasion?
8. Has consideration been given to the method of calling out working parties at short notice, especially at night?
9. How many horses, carts and what tools are available in the locality? (horses and carts in surrounding farms)
10. Is your local Messenger Service adequate, and if more than one, have the personnel been pooled? (2 Messengers in ARP)
11. Are you aware of the Police emergency system of communication?
12. What arrangements have been made when 'stand to' and 'action stations' is received? (would call out Heads of various services)
13. What arrangements have been made for establishing liaison between Defence Committees and local Military Commander after 'action stations'? (would get in touch with CO at Britannia III, The Royal Dart Hotel)
14. Are deputies available, men or women, in the event of principals becoming casualties?
15. What arrangements and method of communication have been made by Chairman for consulting members of Defence Committee after 'stand to'? (an emergency meeting would be immediately called)
16. What arrangements have been made for liaison with adjoining areas and have mutual aid schemes been formed? (liaison with Dartmouth and Brixham would immediately operate)
17. Do all services represented on the Committee realise that they will have to continue to function after isolation?

Quite a lot of food for thought there which would have focused the minds of those involved!

The ARP took part in Invasion Exercises. One such activity took place across Torbay on 30 August 1941 starting at 8pm and finishing at 2pm on Sunday 31 August. All personnel stood by for duty but nothing happened! The active exercise took place in Torquay, Paignton and Brixham. However Mr Stanleick, the baker, provided a box of food for the seventeen personnel who had waited with keen anticipation for action.

The ARP held a dance in the Village Hall on 10 September 1941 in aid of the RAF Pilots and Aircrew Fund. Doors opened at 7.30pm and special permission was needed from Brixham Police for it to finish late at 11pm. Admission was 2/- on the door, and a '3d draw for a basket of fruit was a success' raising £1-17s-6d. Mr Heal 'gave 6 large bottles of mineral refreshment for the concert.' A four man RAF band provided the music and the profit was £8-0s-3d, which would be about £300 today!

The ARP had their offices in the Village Hall. They sported a table and two chairs in the area to the right of the stage. This is about 10ft by 5ft so must have been fairly cosy for more than two at a time! They had a telephone, Kingswear 83, and the map below was on the wall. It shows the static water tanks, a barrage balloon, marks where bombs fell and flags denoting French billets and boats. Lionel Fairweather was in charge of the ARP and was usually contactable at his home or at his garage. The ARP Office was only manned at a time of alarm or raid.

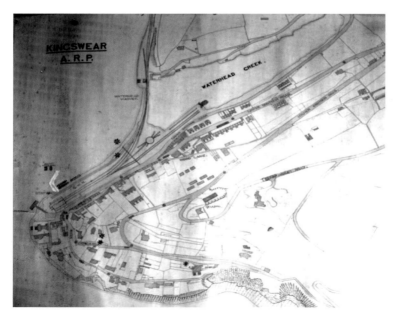

The ARP committee held a meeting in The Ship Inn on Monday 29 October 1941. The points raised were that:

1. All men and women of the Kingswear postal area serving with His Majesty's Forces would receive a Christmas parcel.
2. A flower and vegetable show to be held in the Hall with 20 prizes
3. A dance to be held in the Hall to raise funds
4. A raffle to raise funds
5. The Hall to be blacked out

The Dance on 7 October raised £6-12s-6d at the door, the band cost £1-10s-0d and the Village Hall committee charged 7/6 for the hire of the hall.

On that day a certain Reg Little, aged 14 years and 4 months, volunteered to join the ARP in their messenger service.

A couple of weekends later there was another Invasion Exercise. Enemy troops were to attack Kingswear and Dartmouth and all Civil Defence Services were to be involved. Meetings were held with the ARP and Civil Defence committees, and discussions were held with Mr Bott the Town Clerk of Dartmouth. Details of the proposed exercise came from Brigadier General Gompertz and Mr Fairweather liaised with the Brixham Police.

The exercise assumed that enemy aircraft flew up the estuary at 0900 dropping bombs in the river and on to Britannia III (Royal Dart Hotel). More bombs fell on Belgravia Terrace with multiple casualties (15 teenage boys volunteered to be 'wounded') and blocked the road. By 0920 fifty incendiary bombs had hit Hillside Terrace causing extensive fires with another 100 devices landing around College View wounding two ARP staff. By now one ARP warden had been killed and another wounded at the Belgravia incident. By 1005 more high explosives had landed on the railway sidings with ten casualties, extensive damage to trucks and carriages, 'a matter in hand by GWR staff', and a burst water main. There must have been relief that the exercise ended at 1030!

Mr Fairweather, the exercise umpire, thought the event 'was fairly good, but highlighted the need for an ambulance, and many weaknesses were shown, but those taking part enjoyed the general run of things.'

Mr Jack Bissett, an ARP member and proprietor of the Co-op shop, was married on 14 January 1942 and the rest of the group collected £2-1s-0d towards a wedding present. This was a 'weather glass' and a small brass plate was added with the inscription 'Best wishes from Kingswear ARP 1942'.

The log records that on 12 February they received three air raid alerts. Four unexploded HE bombs fell on Torquay causing casualties, the plane then machine gunned the sea front without further casualties. It was eventually shot down near Exeter.

Ten days later Exercise Drake was held from 0930 to 1730. Again all the staff were expected to be on duty. Happily Mr Stanleick the baker had been hard at work again and produced a large box of sandwiches and cakes (cost £1-6s-3d) and with 'half gallon of milk from the dairy' (1/6) and 'some bottles of beer from Mr Sutton' (£1) thirst was catered for as well.

Dartmouth and Kingswear Warship Week was scheduled for March 1942, the aim being to raise £120,000. Many activities were held on both sides of the river, but the ARP organised a Ball and Cabaret on 19 March in the Village Hall which was 'beautifully decorated with red white and blue streamers'. Mr Sutton had made a model of a destroyer, HMS Haldon, which was fixed across the front of the stage and 'lit up with small bulbs from bow to stern and up to the masthead.' On the wall behind the stage was a large notice declaring 'HMS Haldon £120,000'. The visit of His Worship the Mayor and Mayoress of Dartmouth was much appreciated; they stayed from 9pm until 10.30pm. The cabaret started at 9.30pm and 'was equal to any that could be seen in London.' The dance 'was judged to be the finest ever held in Kingswear.' Tickets were 5/- each with nearly 80 sold but after paying for the band (£6) the cabaret (£8) and hire of the hall (7/6) the profit was £8-12s-9d. The final total for the week was an amazing £128,000. HMS Haldon, a type 2 Hunt class destroyer, was ordered from Fairfields at Glasgow and building started in January 1941.

After some air raid damage whilst under construction, she was eventually launched in April 1942. However as soon as she was completed she was transferred to the Free French fleet and renamed as La Combattante. Amongst many other actions she was involved in the Juno part of the D day landings. She was eventually sunk on 23 February 1945 after hitting a mine off the Humber Estuary that had recently been laid by a German boat. Sixty seven men lost their lives but 118 were saved by two MTBs.

On 13 October 1942 the ARP were delighted to receive their ambulance – it had been on order for three years!

Static water tanks were built in various places around the village. These provided an emergency water supply for fire fighting purposes, although many youngsters enjoyed these new swimming pools! Against all rules of course! Reg Little described the tanks that were fitted around the village, one below Spittis Park, one on the waste ground next to the Co-op (now Zannes cafe), one outside the Church, another opposite Alta Vista (now Nonsuch House) on Church Hill and one next to the air-raid shelter on Ridley Hill. Reg continues that 'they were about 30 feet long 8 feet wide and 5 feet deep and mostly made of steel. One massive one was built of brick in the grounds of the Quarry (now Mount Pleasant flats). This must have been 25' wide and 7' deep. The back wall can still be seen at the back of the flats. Children used to swim in it. The static water tanks were fed by a 6" iron pipe, which ran from Collins' Quay up Church Hill in the left hand side in the gutter up to Ridley Hill and the Quarry. There was another pipe to Fore Street and Spittis Park.' Water from the river was pumped up into the tanks and the Fire Brigade would regularly check the tanks and top up if necessary.

Reg Little remembers that the older Scouts gave their services as messengers and as "casualties" during ARP exercises in the village. The AFS (Auxiliary Fire Service) in Kingswear was formed mostly of Senior Scouts aged about 16. Special permission had to be obtained from the Home Office as they were under the normal age for this service. The person in charge was Mr King who ran the Riversea Hotel in Beacon Road. Other members included Roy Kelland, Raymond Hawke, Nelson Pollard, Ken Allen, Frank and Bert Little, Des and Les Radford, Ted Burrows and Mr Hunt.

The AFS had an American car called a Marquette, which belonged to Lionel Fairweather, the garage owner, and a Beresford trailer pump. They spent a great deal of time putting out fern fires in the railway cutting above the Noss. They also helped put out a fire in HMS Cicala (Royal Dart Hotel) but on this occasion no drivers were available, so they coasted down the road from their garage near the village shop! Later a Nissen hut was built on the roof of the lock-up garages near the village shop, where half the AFS were on duty on alternate nights through out the war.

This is the Kingswear Auxiliary Fire Service in 1940/41 with their Beresford Stork trailer pump. From left to right they are Mr King, Reg Thompson, Ted Mardon, Major Goldsmith, Ted Radford, Jack Eveleigh, Roy Kelland, Raymond Hawke, Harry Richardson, Ted Burrows and Nelson Pollard.

Nelson Pollard became a Petty Officer and for a time worked with Landing Craft although his widow does not remember if he was involved in the D-day landings. His father was a baker and for a time was based in the village bakery in The Square. This is now the ferry office.

Jack Eveleigh remembers that early in the war he joined the Fire Service. The 'Fire Station' at that time was two lock up garages where the Village Stores now is. One garage was for the fire trailer, the other was for the car described as 'very old but powerful'. If you were on duty it was a pretty uncomfortable place to stay until the Nissen hut was built on the roof to provide more welcoming accommodation. Jack recalls that Roy Kelland and Nelson Pollard were also in the squad and were just old enough to drive. Ted Mardon the policeman's son, Jack Eveleigh and Ted Burrows were too young to drive.

If a fire was reported the siren would be sounded and the crew were expected to assemble at the fire station. Jack lived at Sunny Cottage just round the corner from Castella. If more fire crew were needed the car and trailer would drive past the houses of other crew members to rally extra support. On one occasion, at night, Jack was asleep in his box room bedroom at the back of the cottage. The agreed drill was for one crew member to knock on his window with a long pole left outside for the purpose. The knock came and Jack was woken from his sleep. He opened the sash window, knowing that one sash rope had been broken for sometime, but now the other rope broke trapping him in the closed window! The fire brigade now had another job to release him!

On another occasion they were called to Oversteps (now High Springs) where Charlie Bovey the chauffeur and gardener had left a bonfire smouldering. As the Burton bus from Brixham came down Slappers Hill, the driver, a Mr Geddes, noticed the flames and alerted the fire service when he reached Kingswear. The AFS dispatched themselves in haste and rapidly and successfully controlled a minor blaze. They then started to return to the fire station. The old Marquette had a powerful engine but a very feeble drum handbrake that worked on the prop shaft. The driver forgot to release the brake. As they came back along Brixham Road (not the one-way road it is now), Ted Mardon said 'there is an orange light following us.' The handbrake was on fire!

It was soon very obvious that they now had a potentially serious fire to deal with! They stopped next to the horse trough in Brixham Road and with the canvas buckets that were part of their kit they soon doused the flames. The car, in its previous life, had been a saloon but modifications had chopped the body off behind the driver's seat and the area replaced with wooden planks. This allowed ladders to be carried but also proved very flammable! As well as the driver, one or two passengers could travel in the cab but the other crew members stood on these boards holding on to the ladders!

The ARP kept detailed lists of the various local defence groups and this record shows who were the responsible Fire Guards for which area.

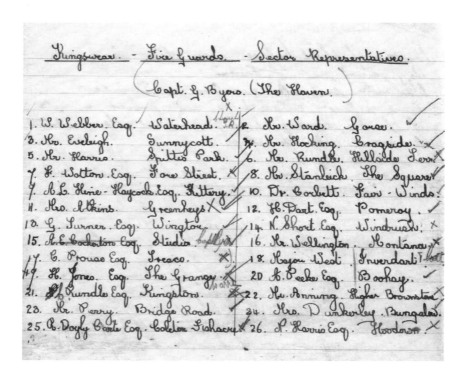

While the list below identifies the precise zone that each Fire Guard would cover:

Fire Guards Sections.

1. Waterhead to Church Park Cottages.
2. Gorse. Brixham Rd to No 1. Brixham Rd. (the Alley)
3. Sunnycott. Longfield. Castella.
4. Esplanade to Kincum Park.
5. Spittis Park to Bottom of Wood Lane.
6. Hillside Terr. to Bottom of Belgravia Steps.
7. Fore St. + Back St. to Entrance of Hall.
8. The Square. Trent Cott.
9. Club to Slittery.
10. Alms Houses to Fair Winds.
11. Greenheys to Bight.
12. Bottom of Church Hill to Alta Vista.
13. Wingtors. Contour Heights to Top of Wood Lane.
14. Hillcrest. to Mount Ridley.
15. Studio + Reservoir Cottages.
16. Gables to Fir Mount. Higher Contour Rd.
17. Woodlane. Top to Bottom.
18. Inverdart, Lodge + Beacon.
19. Grange, Pinewoods, Home Farm, White House, Dower
20. Boohay Hamlet.
21. Kingston.
22. Higher Brownstone.
23. Bridge Rd.
24. Bungalows, Uplands, to Floodown House.
25. Coleton Fishacre including. Farm.
26. Floodown, Oversteps, Cliffland.
27. Cemetry Lodge.

On the 8th of May 1942 the King and Queen arrived at Kingswear at 10:30am for a visit to the college. Lionel Fairweather, representing the Parish Council, and Mr Bovey the Station Master were presented to the King and Queen. When they left at 1pm they thanked Mr Bovey and the Special Constables for the arrangements made at the station.

Anti Aircraft Guns and barrage balloons were fitted after the Noss raid, with several barrages being placed around the area. Reg Little remembers that 'one was at the side of the creek near my parent's house, one was at Noss Point where there used to be allotments. Another was placed at Ballast Cove near Britannia Halt and others on ships in the river. One very windy day the barrage balloon on the creek sidings broke adrift and blew through Kingswear trailing its wire and wrapped itself around the overhead cables supplying both the radar station and Brownstone Battery site. After lunch that day the entire electricity staff had to go up with the RAF balloon experts to unwind it, and re-connect the supply.'

Barrage balloons float over moored warships

He goes on to say that 'Kingswear's defences had by now progressed from a pillbox overlooking the river and railway at Hoodown (still there) to a Nissen Hut and a Bofors Gun in the field hedge above Hoodown House in Hoodown Lane. There was a Bofors Gun at Noss, a Vickers Gun on the riverside by Britannia Halt and barrage balloon in the sidings which now serve as the Marina car park.'

Dick Harris described the actions of the Bofors gun placements on the ridge above Croftlands Farm. During one particular raid two Fokker-Wulf planes were flying over at an extremely low level. The Bofors guns fired away. They were 'pretty hopeless and never hit anything apart from the roof of Kingston Farm', happily causing very little damage as the shell did not explode.'

The Bofors guns were manned by three men in shifts. There would be eight to ten men on site, eating, sleeping and living in Nissen huts adjacent to the guns. These gun sites would be inspected daily by an officer arriving on a motorcycle and occasionally by a senior officer who would come up by Jeep. Dick felt that the main reason for this visit was to stop off at the farm house for a cuppa!

Back row: Ethel Williams, Mr Wallace, Mr Towadrill, Mr Ward, Mr Sharland & son, John Wordsworth, Mr Roberts, Charlie Bovey, Pincher Martin, Jack Thompson
Middle row: Nellie Pocock, Reg Worth, Lionel Fairweather, Henry Kauntz, Harry Williams, Sam Northcott, Miss Oliver
Front row: Norman Weekes, Jack Bissett, Mr Hopper, Reg Little, Charlie Burrows, Roy Sutton

The above photograph was taken on 11 May 1942 by Mr Smale near the entrance to Kingswear School. The entrance to the air raid shelter is behind John Wordsworth (a descendant of the poet!)

After a while Jack Eveleigh became fed up with the Fire Service and joined the Home Guard. One of their principle duties was to patrol the quayside from the jetty to the railway bridge. This would be done in pairs on a two hour on, four hours off basis. Their office and duty room was above the shop, now occupied by Teddy Bears, adjacent to the Post Office in The Square. The patrolling could become tedious at times, so a quick sneak behind the sheds for a crafty smoke was felt very necessary! At other times when off duty they might go to the Working Mens Club in what we now know as the lower Village Hall. The Caretaker Skipper Knowles would charge 6d for half an hour on the snooker table.

Jack provided this photograph of the Kingswear Home Guard on parade outside the goods sheds at the station. He is not in the picture but his brother Jim is wearing his helmet at a rather jaunty angle 7th from the left. Horace Hamlyn is 3rd from the right and was injured in the Noss bombing. The old red fire engine that is currently displayed on the station platform was stored in the back of the goods shed, which has long since been demolished.

On October 7th 1941 Reg Little joined the civil defence as a messenger. After taking a Red Cross exam he became a member of the First Aid Party. By the age of 16 he was a full member of the Rescue Party.

Kingswear Village Hall (telephone number Kingswear 83) as now was a very important community building. It was the venue for many of the WI meetings and was also the Headquarters of all the Civil Defence activities. It was also the dance hall with dances being held in aid of various charities and war efforts. Reg Little recalls that 'money was raised from dances to begin a "Welcome Home" fund for the members of the forces. Each returned serviceman was given a brown leather wallet and a pound note. I was the last one to receive this, as I had been the last person to join up before the war ended.'

Up until March 10th 1941 there had been 260 civil defence alerts involving many of the different groups of volunteers. At that time in the Kingswear postal area there were:

150 Fire Watchers
22 Special Police
15 Red Cross Nurses
18 National Fire Service
22 Air Raid Wardens
8 Rest Centre Workers (Wesleyan school room)
20 Members of Defence Committee
8 Members of the First Aid Party
8 Members of the Rescue Party
2 Doctors in the village
57 Stirrup pumps issued
28 - the total number of cars in the parish!
85 Servicemen returned and they were sent Christmas Cards each year by the Civil Defence Committee.

'At the end of the war the Civil Defence Members who had served 3 years were awarded the Defence Medal. I was pleased to be so honoured' said Reg Little.

Mrs Heal from the barber and tobacconist shop had a full schedule too. As well as three children, she took in two evacuated girls from Eltham in London. Later there were two RAF men (one was called Bob, and he came from Bournemouth. Margaret Heal took a holiday with Bob and his wife after the war) and two WAAF girls, one called Daphne. Fortunately the house had five large bedrooms. Mrs Heal was required to provide dinner, bed and breakfast for the billeted troops, for which she received a weekly fee. She would also have needed their ration books in order to buy enough food. The family and lodgers would all eat together around the dining table which doubled up as an air raid shelter of the Morrison type. She remembers her mother as 'a good cook' who 'always produced a good meal' although they all missed fruit which was very difficult to obtain. Dried and tinned fruit was a real luxury. Meat was also heavily rationed but local farmers went door to door offering rabbits for 'about a shilling.' Mrs Heal would skin and gut them and was able to sell the skins 'for a pittance' to a man who came to the door.

The photograph above shows Charlie Heal outside his shop in The Square, and below shows Margaret Heal with her brother in front of the shop door which now leads into the Post Office.

Sir David Clayton remembers that his father, Lt-Commander Arthur Clayton RNVR, was based in Kingswear during the war. Occasionally he would stay with his father who lived at Combe Bank in Brixham, then a grand house in two acres but now a collection of sheltered flats and apartments. He was Commodore to Brixham Yacht Club and a designer of boats. David Clayton recalls successfully racing one of his father's boats 50 years later!

Arthur Clayton was the oldest skipper of coastal forces vessels and responsible for a D boat. This was a class of 115ft long motor gun boats, some of which were later fitted with torpedo tubes. There were frequent raids to the north Brittany coast, crossing at night and attacking German convoys.

The Fairmile D-class Motor Torpedo Boat displaced 90 tons, was 115ft long with a beam of 21ft but only drawing 5ft. Varying specifications would affect the overall weight which could creep up to 120 tons. They were prefabricated boats which could be finally assembled in small shipyards that were more used to building pleasure craft. They could be powered by four Packard petrol engines giving a top speed of 27 knots and a range of 2000 miles at more modest speeds. Other engines were also used in these fast coastal vessels. It was at this time that the torpedo jetty, workshops and oil tanks were built at Hoodown to help service the MGBs and MTBs.

Royal Navy Officers and Seamen were usually found on the vessels of the main naval fleet but crews for these smaller boats would often be drawn from Royal Naval Volunteer Reserve personnel such as Arthur Clayton. They were, not surprisingly, extremely proud to be allowed command of their own vessel. They were soon involved in some of the bravest missions imaginable.

David Clayton recalls the report that Lt-Commander Clayton had a wind up gramophone with large trumpet loud speaker on the deck of his D-class, and would play 'a hunting we will go' as they motored out of the Dart!

It was also said that he would 'clear the guns out' as he was leaving the Dart using the Mewstone as target practice! Is the rock not quite as tall as it once was?

Arthur Clayton was very proud of his vessel and wanted to show it to an uncle who lived near Salcombe. The Admiral made it very clear to him that he must NOT take his vessel into Salcombe in view of the sand bar.

One occasion when he was very near Salcombe he became aware of a Spitfire in distress and crashing into the sea. They made full speed to the area, and managed to rescue the pilot who was badly burned. It was clear that he needed urgent hospital treatment. Salcombe offered the only realistic hope for the wounded airman. At that time there was just enough water to get into Salcombe over the bar and alongside to offload the pilot who was safely transferred to hospital, saving his life. It was now necessary to tell the Admiral that they were in Salcombe; his response was unrepeatable. However, the circumstances were accepted in view of the life saved. The Admiral was then told that they would be staying there until the next high tide!

These crews often had to undertake secret missions. Many of these amazing stories can be read in Lloyd Bott's *The Secret War from the River Dart*. On one occasion they were instructed to patrol their part of the channel and, as no other allied shipping would be in the area, they should vigorously attack any other vessel they encountered. A little later the eerie shape of a large ship appeared out of the gloom. Fingers were poised on triggers and hands on torpedo levers ready for the kill. At the last moment Commander Clayton recognised the silhouette of HMS Ajax, pride of the Royal Navy, which was also on a secret mission! Arthur Clayton's sharp thinking and excellent ship recognition ensured that a very costly blunder was averted!

Topline Broadhurst was awarded his first commission at the age of 21 in Coastal Forces on the ageing MGB 57, based in Weymouth. It was powered by 3 Rolls Royce Merlin engines similar to the Spitfire engine, but the gorgeous sound was muffled by the water. Three throttles, one for each engine, were in front of him on the bridge. Topline, with great joy in his voice, describes the adrenaline rush and thrill of pushing all three throttles forward together, the engines roaring to maximum power, the stern dipping back into the water and the boat rushing forward to top speed. Whilst chasing E boats in Lyme Bay in heavy seas, the MGB crashed repeatedly into the waves until a part of a chine fell off. Chines are longitudinal strips on a hull that help deflect down the water spray. A hull may have 2 or more chines to approximate a round bottomed shape with flat panels. They limped back to Uphams yard in Brixham where the boat was cradled out of the water. The damage proved to be more extensive than first thought and the boat was declared scrap. His next vessel was MGB 112 armed with 0.5in machine guns either side of the bridge, Oerlikon guns, firing 20mm shells, fore and aft and 2 depth charges.

Topline's flotilla, consisting of eight boats, was based in the Dart and moored alongside an old tramp steamer in the middle of the river. The crew would be based on the MGB with their mess and washing facilities on the tramp steamer. The two officers on each boat were based at The Royal Dart Hotel. The first floor and balcony were the Mess with the floors above for bedrooms. Topline remembers being well fed in the Mess, with adequate time to enjoy his favoured Plymouth gin. They then needed more space and took over initially Longford, and then Kittery Court. It was his task to approach Mr Hine-Haycock to explain that their spare rooms were about to be invaded! This was initially met, not surprisingly, with considerable resistance. Latterly, however, the Hine-Haycocks agreed how much they had enjoyed the youthful company!

Almost all their sorties were at nighttime. Crossing the channel in daylight would have made them easy targets for German planes, and rough seas were also a no-go area. In calm waters, however, his boat was fast and manoeuvrable. The MGB would cruise at 30 knots and have a maximum speed of 45 knots, and a night's cruising would guzzle 2000 gallons of petrol! Standing above a tank of 2000 gallons of petrol must have focussed the mind, perhaps even more so when Topline knew that the German E boats ran on the much less volatile diesel!

One Christmas night after a good session in the pub they were told that they had to take a trip across the channel! Their task was to take a group of army soldiers to Guernsey; they were picked up from Dartmouth carrying wicker shopping baskets filled with hand grenades! They sailed across the channel at night with muffled exhausts to reduce the chance of being heard. They stopped about 1000 yards from the shore to allow the soldiers to complete their journey by inflatable dinghy. The soldiers would have to give a very definite time by which they would be back on the MGB, if they were late the boat had to leave without them to be able to get back to Dartmouth before daylight. On this occasion the soldiers were indeed back in good time but came with two guests! They had surprised two German soldiers who were taken prisoner still dressed in their night shirts! They probably did not enjoy their trip to England carefully tucked up below decks.

Topline recalls taking plenty of sandwiches and fruit on these sorties, with large thermos flasks of soup or coffee or even occasionally filled with gin! When back in the Dart, parties were a regular feature. But how did you know which boat was hosting the party? The officer's quarters were on the port side of an MGB so the boat heeling that way was the one to aim for! Even the harbourmaster joined in, at least until he had to be dragged from the river a little the worse for drink!

A flotilla of MGBs coming back into the river must have been an awesome sight, especially if the temptation of a gin or a party caused the fleet to maintain excessive speed. The wash from the boats then became significant. On one occasion, a group of ladies on the lower ferry pontoon, returning from Dartmouth with their shopping, got thoroughly wet feet as the wash flowed right across the flat deck of the pontoon! Nice ladies do not usually swear at young officers. This episode, however, was not usual!

The intentions of the Naval Forces were I am sure, never in doubt. However they could sometimes be clumsy! A destroyer was moored for the night adjacent to the Higher Ferry. As it was leaving the next morning, its anchor managed to drag and break the main electricity cable running from Dartmouth to Kingswear! It was a week before Kingswear had a full supply again!

American construction engineers widened Bridge Road down to the Higher Ferry from its previous single track with passing places. Workshops were built at Britannia Crossing with repair facilities, and guns were fitted on the railway embankment above and below the crossing. Landing craft were continuously coming into the river and this was the first time that Sheila Little had seen the amphibious DUKW craft driving down Bridge Road, into the water and up a ramp onto the landing craft. Mrs Brodie, the ferry manager's wife, was seen running after them in a panic and calling 'have you got your ticket?' DUKWs were all-wheel drive amphibious trucks designed by General Motors in USA. (D indicates that it was designed in 1942, U meant utility, K indicated all-wheel drive and the W indicated two powered rear axles, apparently).

This photograph shows American Landing craft with Kingswear in the background and moored vessels in the river. The Higher Ferry slipway on the Kingswear side was modified to allow landing craft to load on that side of the river as well.

References
Lloyd Bott's *The Secret War from the River Dart*.
Paul Moynagh 2006 Kingswear Historians Newsletter
Reg Little - Growing up in Wartime Kingswear
Wikipedia on DUKWs and MGBs
The Marquette Society
Gordon Thomas' photograph archive

8. The Motor Boats

The Royal Dart Hotel, adjacent to the lower ferry's slipway, was taken over, in part, by the Royal Navy in 1943 and initially called HMS Dartmouth II. At this stage Britannia Royal Naval College was called HMS Dartmouth III. The Hotel later was renamed HMS Cicala.

The Motor Torpedo Boat flotilla began to arrive on the Dart, and, supported by HMS Belfort was stationed at Forwood's Wharf at Hoodown where the Dart Harbour Navigation Authority now has its workshop. Torpedoes were also stored here with fuel stores for the MTBs in tanks at the end of Waterhead Creek. The torpedo tubes were built at Kingswear Court with the car ferries used to transport materials.

Sir Harold Clayton (second from left) inspecting boys at the Brixham Boys Home, now Grenville House

Sir Arthur, who was the oldest skipper of coastal forces vessels, was in charge of one of the Fairmile D boats as described earlier. They were 115ft long with a beam of just less than 21ft and an open bridge; not a lot of fun in a February blizzard! The four Packhard petrol engines delivered 5000hp and gave a very good turn of speed. They had a crew of twenty one. Motor Gun Boats were very much inshore defence vessels, some being later converted to Motor Torpedo Boats. Later in the war, MTBs were being built specifically for that role. The hulls were wooden and built in sections. They were then transported by lorry to a shipyard where they could be bolted together and then fitted out. Sir Arthur's boat was MTB 677. They would make frequent raids to the north Brittany coast, crossing at night and attacking German convoys. They sometimes had to drop 'pongos' or 'brown jobs' (Naval slang for soldiers!) off onto French soil, and were known to come back with German prisoners.

MTB 677 at speed in the Channel

Sir Arthur Clayton on the bridge of MTB 677 with Coxswain Skinner

A Memorial Service was held for Sir Arthur Harold Clayton at Kingswear Church on Tuesday 24 September 1985. An address was given by Topline Broadhurst as follows;

ADDRESS BY TOPLINE BROADHURST FOR THE MEMORIAL SERVICE FOR SIR ARTHUR HAROLD CLAYTON. Bart., D.S.C. ST.THOMAS OF CANTERBURY CHURCH, KINGSWEAR, DEVON. TUESDAY, 24th SEPTEMBER, 1985.

If any proof was needed of the love and friendship in which Arthur was held by both young and old alike, we have it today, in this lovely church, where so many have travelled great distances to be here.

I'm here because I first met Arthur forty-three years ago when we were setting ready for the Dieppe Raid.   We were both in command of Motor Gun Boats, but Arthur was senior to me and I was ordered to tie up my small boat along side his larger one anchored in the Solent. I was just going to report my presence, when a cheery face with a large grin appeared in the chartroom doorway.

"I'm Arthur. Come aboard and have a gin and let's talk about this party we're going on".

Arthur was the last person in the world to stand on ceremony or be pompous, and it was a very long time indeed before I learnt that he was to eventually become "Sir Arthur", the 11th baronet in a long line of Claytons going back to 1732.

At that time, I had no idea that one day I would meet his father, his children and his grandchildren, and get to know some of the family really very well, because in those days one didn't look too far ahead. But we met up again in 1943 when he brought his MGB here to Kingswear for Special Duties.

He had the unenviable task of taking parties of Special Service Soldiers to land on the enemy occupied coasts of France and the Channel Islands, and the soldiers would come aboard with wicker shopping baskets, full of hand grenades. When Arthur got as close as he could to the enemy held shore, the soldiers would go off into the darkness in their rubber dinghies. Arthur would then have to wait to hopefully rendezvous with them several hours later. Not a very pleasant job, so close to the enemy coast, but Arthur didn't turn a hair, and was delighted one night when some German prisoners were brought back in their night-shirts, protesting loudly. And if it turned a bit rough on the way home, he reveled in it as he tucked into fried eggs and bacon when some of the others couldn't look at them. Although we didn't know it, this was all in preparation for 'D-Day' and Arthur was promoted to a larger boat with torpedoes, MTB 677, and it was then that he was "Mentioned in Dispatches" as the citation says:-

"As Commanding Officer of MTB 677, forming part of the force which torpedoed and damaged an Elbing class destroyer on the nights of 6/7 May 1944 he handled his ship with considerable skill and coolness, less than one mile from the enemy coast in conditions of bright moonlight, and a swell in shallow waters surrounded by rocks dangerous to navigation. He maneuvered his ship, undetected by the enemy, into the correct position, and had it been necessary for him to fire torpedoes, would have been able to do so with a good chance of hitting the target."

And any of you who have sailed over to the north coast of Brittany will know what a treacherous coast it is, even in daylight, but just imagine what it would have been like in 1944, and at night.

A little later, Arthur was awarded the Distinguished Service Cross. The citation reads:

"For bravery and skill in command of MTB 677 when in actions against the enemy on the nights of 26/27 June and 5/6 August 1944. In these actions, MTB 677 inflicted considerable damage on the enemy. This Commanding Officer is a keen and efficient seaman who has been an inspiration to his ship's company and an example to the Flotilla."

The bald facts of the citation do not mention the severity of the damage suffered by MTB 677 or of the fire aft and the fact that Arthur was standing on top of over two thousand gallons of high octane petrol! In these actions, our MTB's were attacking very much larger and more heavily armed enemy minesweepers and trawlers as well as E-Boats, and it's worth remembering that Arthur was now forty years old and a lot older than the other officers in command of our MTB's as they moved up the English Channel, helping to bottle up the German Navy, night after night, to keep the supply routes open for our advancing army, and he finally finished up in Dover and then Ramsgate.

No doubt a very exhilarating time for Arthur, but a very tiring and taxing period with no let up at all, but in fact, he often nonchalantly referred to all this as "Yachting at the Government's expense".

After the war, he eventually came back to the river he loved, and took a very active part in helping the R.N.L.I, by collecting funds for the Brixham boat, just as his father had done and following in his grandfather's footsteps, who was National Chairman of the R.N.L.I.

He also realized the value of keeping the local hospital going at Brixham and did great work on the committee of the League of Friends. He ran the flag days very successfully. For many years he also helped with that very necessary and welcome service of "Meals on Wheels", and his cheery self was much appreciated by those he regularly visited.

He loved sailing and did a lot to help with the Junior Sailing Organisation. Once his active days of sailing were over, you could see a long line of boats being towed up river, and you'd know that Arthur was at the head of them, still doing what he could to help.

During the war, Arthur cooperated with the American Torpedo Boats - PT Boats, as they were called - and in 1966 he was invited to America and given the Freedom of the City of New Orleans, in recognition of the help and good work that he had done during the war, and I know that he was very touched by this unique honour.

Often, as one gets older, one gets more lonely. But Arthur had the good fortune to 'marry the girl next door', if I may put it that way, and so acquired a whole new family for the last twenty years of his life, and it was particularly noticeable how the young loved him and how popular he was with them, and how happy he was during this time.

I last saw him shortly before he died, and he had the same broad grin and a twinkle in his eyes as he looked at the pictures of his MTB 677, hanging on the walls of his room, overlooking the beautiful Dart River. I'm sure Arthur will never be far away from the River he loved so much, - but for us, we sadly know, that as we climb the steep Kingswear Hill, no longer will that cheery face with a broad grin be there to greet us - and we shall greatly miss a friend - and a true English Gentleman.'

Topline Broadhurst was in the 8th Flotilla Gunboats and recalls that the officers were ferried out from their HQ at HMS Cicala to mid-river where their MGBs were tied up alongside an old tramp steamer. Refuelling was adjacent to Hoodown and the torpedo store was in a shed on the site of the Dartmouth Harbour Navigation Authority workshop.

Sheila Little writes 'during the school holidays I went to Dittisham with a friend to visit his grandmother. His father was the shipyard manager at Galmpton where MLs and MGBs were being built. We were shown all round the partly built boats.

I remember being shown the self sealing fuel tanks with a special outer layer. These were the boats used in the Secret Fleet.'

Reg and Sheila recount the story of the Secret Fleet in 'Growing up in Wartime Kingswear': 'In 1942, in the middle of the river just above Hoodown, a large paddle steamer was moored. Alongside were several MTBs and MGBs. We saw them coming and going and aroused no interest, as we thought they were part of the main flotilla. In the late 1960s there was great surprise when we learnt that the boats had comprised "The Secret Fleet".

On dark nights they had set off for Brittany, some 80 miles away, where they anchored off a remote beach. They were guided in by a 16 year old girl, who sometimes had to stand waist deep in water, signaling to the boat with a torch. They would stop some distance off shore as there were German fortifications near the landing point. They would row in to the rough, rocky shore with great care in special boats. Silence was essential. The young girl, who was awarded both French and British decorations after the war, guided crashed and shot-down airmen, escaped prisoners, and agents through a minefield and down a cliff to the shore.

On the beach they met radio operators, Special Operations Executive members and men and women of the Maquis (French Resistance) who had come across from the Dart with other specialist equipment. This was to interfere in every way possible with the enemy. It is not known by many that the post war President of France, Francois Mitterand — said by some to be a collaborator, as he was a member of the Retain government - was brought into the Dart and went up to London and back via the Secret Fleet. All of the men and women, who were brought back, were put quietly on the train at Kingswear. They travelled in special locked compartments on the 8.05am train and were met at Paddington and taken for de-briefing.

On the trip a few days prior to D-Day, eighty two downed pilots and aircrew were returned from France. They were mixed American and British flyers and were urgently required for service after D-Day.

None of us who lived here at the time knew that any of this was happening. People knew how to keep their mouths shut in those days. Members of the Flotilla were the most decorated group of servicemen ever to go to The Palace at the end of the war.

MGB 502

Alfred F. Harris was a crew member and Seaman Gunner on MGB 502 as part of the 15th Flotilla Special Service. He wrote the following poem describing his feelings on the secret missions. It is part of a collection of thoughts and photographs assembled by Major Dick Parkes and now in the archives of Kingswear Historians.

NIGHT MISSION 1944

Sombre and sleek she slipped through the water
Closing the enemy occupied shore
Poised to evade the many that sought her
HM motor gun boat was fighting her war

Low silhouette and camouflaged paintwork
Special her purpose and secret her plan
Cloaked by the night and dark sea around her
On smooth silent engines so softly she ran

Action stations with eyes ever watchful
Men sought the white of an enemy wake
Down in the waist the boats' crews were gathered
Stowing the gear that the small boats would take

Reducing speed now stop both the engines
Starting to roll as she slowly lost way
Charthouse and bridge both checking position
Sure to locate the right spot in the bay

Glasses to shoreward watch for the signal
Green glow that briefly shines through the night
Small boats are outboard in go the seamen
Setting their course for the faint distant light

Clear the ships side with a pull on the sweep oar
Give way together, start in on the run
Muffled and greased the oars in their crutches
Bowman and stroke oar dipping as one

Feel the surf catch her and race for the shoreline
Out boat the oarsman, feet grip the sand
Turn her bows seaward hold fast to gunwales
Senses alert for the danger at hand

Whisper of voices, forms in the darkness
Quickly the cargo is moved up the beach
Crunch of feet running, American airman
Head for the small boats packed tightly in each

Into the surf with the boats overladen
Heavy the pull with the oars digging deep
Seeing the mother ship loom from the blackness
Up ropes and scrambling nets hanging so steep

Lash up the small boats set course for England
Feel the winds bite through soaking wet clothes
Welcome the dawn and first sight of Dartmouth
Rig ship for port side to, all engines slow.

Andrew Smith (left in photograph) was First Lieutenant on MGB 503 and Lloyd Bott (on the right) Lieutenant on MGB 502 respectively. Lloyd Bott described MGBs as 'small but serious vessels of war'. Their boats were unusual as they were the only such vessels in the Navy to be diesel powered, each with three 1500hp silenced engines. They could cruise at 21 knots for 1000 miles and achieve 30 knots for short bursts. The 15th Flotilla was moored mid stream behind them in the River Dart, alongside Westward Ho, an old tramp steamer.

This photograph shows MGBs 502 and 503 moored alongside Westward Ho.

Sheila Little also recalls that 'mines on railway wagons on the jetty were loaded onto a minelayer. I understood that they were laid across the harbour entrance some distance out. About this time a small boat was picked up by a destroyer just outside the harbour. This was the Ragamuffin. The occupant had been rowing for five days from Jersey after running out of petrol. He then joined the RAF but on his first leave he came back to his boat for a fishing trip to find he had been charged a fee for Import Duty!'

The Museum in Jersey still has this tiny rowboat. It belonged to 21-year-old Denis Vibert. "Denis escaped, rowing all the way to England where HM Customs charged him 10 shillings import duty for the boat" the Museum website explains.

Margaret Rickard remembers that leading up to D day there was a real bustle in the river and the two towns. People were aware that 'something big was going to happen' but did not know what or could not say. The evening before the Normandy invasion she remembers looking out of her bedroom windows at dusk to see boats 'in their hundreds' leaving the Dart. There was 'a strange emptiness' the next morning to see the river deserted and an eerie calmness. Kingswear was never quite the same again.

A river scene viewed from Kingswear Wood before D day.

References:
Sir David Clayton for many photographs and documents
"The Royal Navy's 15th MGB Flotilla" by Lloyd Bott CBE DSC
Gordon Thomas' photo archive

9. The Free French

Tony Higgins has written a book on the Free French 23rd MTB flotilla and has kindly allowed me to include some excerpts here.

There was a Free French naval presence in the area from the time of the fall of France. Two tugs, L'Isere and L'Aube sailed here after Dunkirk and operated in the river throughout the War. Apart from French built vessels, the reformed French Navy was equipped with British built vessels from destroyers down to small coastal craft and mainly based around the east and south coasts. The river Dart was the home of several units of Coastal Forces operating in the Channel.

The origins of the 23rd. MTB Flotilla were in 1941 when the FNFL (Forces Navales Franchises Libres) manned four Motor Launches. This unit formed the 2nd Division of the 20th ML Flotilla, which was based at Portland; the First Division being British manned and subsequently lost all its boats during the attack on St. Nazaire on the 28th March 1942. The flotilla was mainly engaged in coastal escort duties, defensive patrols and air-sea rescue.

The crews provided the nucleus of manpower for the newly formed 23rd Flotilla in 1942 which were then equipped with new Motor Torpedo Boats. After four weeks of "working up" in Weymouth, the boats and crews were then deemed fit to undertake operational duties.

On the 18th January, the Flotilla was inspected by General de Gaulle, who was accompanied by the head of Free French Naval Forces, Admiral Auboyneau. Due to the General's height the requisite size of oilskins were difficult to find but eventually extra large ones were obtained and the distinguished visitors embarked for an inspection at sea. After dinner at the Gloucester Hotel in Weymouth the General and his staff returned to London.

The advance party of the 23rd Flotilla arrived in Kingswear in January 1943. Their HQ was Brookhill, an imposing house overlooking the Dart which looks very much the same today as it did fifty years ago. The first night was spent at the Redoubt, which at the time housed Royal Navy and Royal Marine personnel. The Officers were subsequently billeted at Longford, the crews being housed at Brookhill, Kingswear Court and several other private billets. The Royal Dart Hotel was the HQ of the local Royal Navy shore base bearing the rather grand title of HMS Cicala. It was from here that overall operational command of the 23rd and other Coastal Force units in the area was exercised. The name, but not its location or usage must have been known to the Germans as it was referred to in a radio broadcast by the propagandist William Joyce, more commonly known to the people of Britain as "Lord Haw Haw". When commenting on damage inflicted on Dartmouth by German bombers he proudly informed his listeners that HMS Cicala had also been sunk!

Initially, the Flotilla was commanded by Capitaine de Corvette Meurville and later by Lieutenant Lehle. Three British Liaison Officers, who were fluent French speakers, served with the Unit. None were regular Naval Officers, all being Lieutenants in the RNVR. In addition to the British LOs, Royal Navy telegraphists also served aboard the boats. They wore R.N. uniform and were under command of the LOs for administrative and discipline purposes. During operations they came under the command of French Officers. British ratings over the age of 18 were eligible for a daily rum ration if aboard a RN ship flying the white ensign. This did not apply to the 23rd and the ratings imbibed in the same fashion as their French shipmates, half a litre of vin ordinaire each day, usually taken with their meals.

In February 1943 the first of the boats arrived from Weymouth. The vessels were 72 foot Vosper designed Motor Torpedo Boats, their overall fully loaded displacement being 60 tons. They were powered by three 1200 bhp Packard engines, plus two Ford 75 bhp auxiliary engines. These gave a theoretical maximum speed of 40 knots and a range of 420 miles. The boats' performances and fuel consumption varied considerably, depending on the sea conditions encountered at the time. They carried 2500 gallons of 100 octane petrol. Armament consisted of 2 x 21" torpedoes, 1 x 20mm Oerlikon, 1 x twin 0.5" Vickers (later replaced by a twin Oerlikon) and twin 0.303 machine guns. Other weapons were Lanchester carbines, hand grenades, depth charges and a smoke screen apparatus. The crew was captain, midshipman, coxswain, signalman, torpedo man, two gunners, two radar operators, two radio operators and three motor mechanics.

The depot ship Belfort was originally built as a sloop in the Naval Dockyard of L'Orient in 1919. She was later converted to a seaplane tender and subsequently as a depot ship in a UK shipyard. The Flotilla moored at the jetty which is presently used by the Dart Harbour & Navigation Authority. Torpedoes were stored in the green Nissen hut which today is the workshops of the Authority. 100 Octane fuel was stored in four tanks which were sited below Hoodown House, the fuel being gravity fed to the jetty.

The photograph below was taken by Mr Bovey and shows three MTBs alongside Belfort with the Golf Club House in the background.

From the time of their arrival in Kingswear, exercises were carried out continuously between Start Point and Teignmouth and on the 6th March the first operational sortie took place. At 1725 hrs four of the boats slipped their moorings and headed to the coast of France at a steady 22 knots. Unfortunately at 2130 hours MTB 227 sustained a fire in the engine room and was forced to return to base. The remainder pressed on, alternately changing their position and waiting in silence for a target to appear. The night passed without incident and the Flotilla returned to Kingswear the following day.

The first success came on the 10th March to MTBs 94 and 96. After an all night vigil and shortly before the sortie was about to be called off, a German vessel of approximately 2000 tons together with an escort was spotted. MTB 96 created a diversion by attacking at high speed, firing all her guns at the target. Both vessels replied, the Germans firing star shells which illuminated the attacker. Meanwhile MTB 94 approached the freighter from the opposite direction in darkness and fired her torpedoes. Both hit the target and the bow of the German ship was seen to rise out of the water shortly before it slipped beneath the waves.

Many patrols were uneventful but were nonetheless quite stressful for the crews. Weather conditions were varied, ranging from very rough to flat calm and visibility from a bright moonlit night to thick fog. On the 16th April, off Ushant and in pitch darkness, an RAF pilot who had bailed out of his plane was miraculously located and rescued.

On the 5th May a large enemy force was encountered near the Sept Iles. Torpedoes were fired which missed their targets and resulted in heavy accurate gunfire being directed against the attackers. Much damage was sustained by the boats, many sailors being wounded. One boat limped back with 73 bullet holes in the hull and its bows a metre below the water line. In order to prevent it sinking it was immediately beached on the slipway when it arrived at Kingswear. On the 10th September, South of Guernsey, an enemy convoy was spotted. A furious battle ensued in which an escorting German trawler was hit by a torpedo but unfortunately due to poor visibility and offensive enemy action it could not be ascertained whether the vessel was actually sunk.

On the 11th October near the L'Ile Vierge, two MTBs met two German E boats head on. After a sharp skirmish, both adversaries withdrew without damage. On the 26th December two German E boats were damaged by British cruisers and were reported heading for Brest, The 23rd were ordered to intercept the damaged boats but although they waited in ambush until the morning nothing was spotted. Being so near the French coast in daylight left the Flotilla prone to attack and they were escorted across the channel by RAF Spitfires. On this sortie, crews had been at 'action stations' for a continuous period of 26 hours.

The growing strength of the British Coastal Forces, which were attacking convoys off the occupied mainland from the North Dutch coast to Brittany, brought a not unexpected response from the enemy. The number of escort ships was increased and the firepower of all German vessels upgraded to more accurate guns with larger calibres. By the close of 1943 it became increasingly difficult for the allies to mount successful attacks. On the 31st January a convoy was attacked, but such was the volume of heavy fire brought to bear on the Flotilla that it was not possible to close the range for a torpedo attack and it was fortunate that the boats escaped unscathed.

On the 20th March 1944 three boats from the Flotilla in a joint operation with three 'D' type British MTBs were attacked by a large force of enemy vessels. This battle was unique inasmuch as this was the first time that they had been fired on by enemy shore batteries. All allied vessels were once again fortunate to escape without incurring damage.

The disappointment of so many unsuccessful encounters was erased on the night of the 8th May when fortune once again favoured the 23rd. MTBs which were patrolling in pairs off the coast of Jersey. It was not a good night for an attack. There was a full moon, the visibility being excellent and a still easterly breeze brought showers of spray onto the decks and bridges of the boats. Near midnight, a convoy was spotted. This comprised a cargo vessel of about 3000 tons and a smaller one of about 1500 tons. It was heading in a northerly direction and it was assumed that its destination was Cherbourg. There were no less than eight escorts for these two ships, which was quite a formidable defence. Nevertheless, the decision was made to attack the larger vessel, the biggest problem being the good visibility and the need to close to 800 yards which was an effective range for torpedoes. It was decided to cross the stern of the convoy and then attack from the starboard side. This manoeuvre was carried out at a distance to avoid detection.

Suddenly the whole situation changed when the convoy altered direction with the obvious intention of entering St. Peter Port. It was realised that the only hope of success was to attack immediately. Two boats created a diversion by opening up their engines, which soon trailed white turbulent wakes behind them, and closed on the convoy at high speed. This was soon spotted by the enemy who rained shot and shell on them. The other two boats meanwhile crept in from a dark background and were able to fire their torpedoes. An immense column of smoke and flame erupted from the target and when it had cleared the ship had disappeared. All boats were now under attack and once again shore batteries, this time sited on Guernsey, had them in their sights. MTB 227 had its Vickers turret put out of action; the gunner inside fortunately escaping injury. Two shells also hit the engine room which started a fire. Under the protection of a smokescreen the engine was restarted and the MTB was able to limp away from the fray.

The remaining MTBs mounted a second attack but were driven off. By this time the second cargo vessel had entered the port and was safe. Three of the escorts however were stopped at the entrance picking up survivors from the sunken vessel and it was decided to attack again. Due to the strong possibility that these vessels would soon disappear into the harbour, torpedoes were fired at a greater distance than usual. The range was about 2000 metres and to everyone's relief an escort vessel was seen to explode. The MTBs then closed at 30 knots shooting up the last escort before it could enter the safety of the port. This was not the end of the matter. During the battle it had been observed that a large balloon, tethered by a steel cable to the seabed, was sited near the harbour entrance. It must have been inflated with a combustible gas, as a burst of machine gun fire quickly reduced it to a flaming mass. What was not realised was that the balloon was manned. As it fell to the water a body was also seen falling and later cries were heard from the water. As a result of this action all four boats had the Ordre de L'Armee conferred on them by General de Gaulle. This is a French decoration for bravery awarded to a ship. There is no equivalent award in the British Navy.

A similar sortie in the same area took place on the 13th May. On this occasion the Germans were waiting for them. The Flotilla had damaged a small patrol vessel with gunfire just outside the port, when a superior force of enemy vessels attacked. Only by weaving and dodging at maximum speed were the boats able to make their escape.

A week later on the evening of 19th May four boats were dispatched to a spot six miles west of La Corbiere. Information received indicated that three German MTBs had left Brest on passage to Cherbourg and were likely to pass this spot. The instructions were that the 23rd was to lie in ambush for them. They were also instructed to ignore all other vessels until 0300 hrs after which any targets would be of their own choosing. The four boats split into two pairs and waited. At about 0130 hrs the radar operators reported echoes from four ships about

resolution has been passed in France that a Silver Medal and
Diploma has been awarded to Kingswear in permanent acknowledgement
of the hospitality extended to French Forces.

The French Embassy have asked the Consular Attache and his
wife and a representative of the French Naval Attache's Office
in London to come to the Parish to take part in an official
ceremony when presentations will be made and accepted on behalf
of the parishioners. It is suggested by the Embassy that this
official visit take place either in May or June. My Council
propose to set up a sub-Committee to go into the arrangements
made. They would naturally like you to serve on this Committee
especially as we should like you to take part in it.

Perhaps you will kindly let me know if you are prepared to
accept, I will then arrange to send to you notice of the first
meeting when it is convened.

Kind regards.

Yours sincerely,

Clerk to the Council.

The following description of life based in Kingswear through French eyes comes
from the Archive Department of the Naval War Records office in Cherbourg. It
was translated by Sheila Little.

The writer explains: 'The war presented various ups and downs in an otherwise
well-regulated life. A base for the ships was established in the Dart estuary and
the coastal forces took over the station hotel at Kingswear (The Royal Dart
Hotel). The French officers were billeted at Longford, a delicious little house
surrounded with bushes. It had large bay windows and a terrace overlooking
the waters of the Dart. From there could be seen the boats surrounding the
supply ship Belfort. They were clustered like chicks around a mother hen.

During the day ships were frequently alongside the jetty and the torpedo shed
on the quay; work was done on the torpedoes and tubes, tanks were filled with
fuel. They were in charge of a Master Engineer Mechanic, whom they consulted
about all difficulties. As for the French crews, they were housed at Brookhill,
twenty minutes from the village near the mouth of the Dart. Brookhill was a
large house, lost in the midst of a 3km long park full of ancient trees. At the
door a sailor mounted guard beside a Free French Flag - the Cross of Lorraine.
In the front of the house a beautiful terrace and carved balcony faced the river,
many beautiful parasol pine trees giving the impression of scenery in many

parts of France. In spring, banks of flowers bloomed throughout the garden and the multicoloured blooms brightened the rooms of the officers and men.

We were night-birds. Darkness protected us during the chase and gave us the element of surprise. In winter we used to set off at slow speed in the afternoons, an hour or two before sunset, we arrived as night was falling off the north coast of Brittany. When we re-entered the base dawn was breaking over the mouth of the Dart. At this time in Dartmouth, as in other parts of Great Britain, one didn't see much of women, but there were WRNS (Women's Royal Naval Service or Wrens as they were known) in their blue uniforms who had plenty to do with all their duties, mounting guard, sending and receiving signals etc., There were others who served breakfast, helped with repairs and cleaning, and with first aid for minor injuries.

Like night birds, we slept during the day and woke up at night to coincide with the movements of the enemy. Leisure time was sacred to music (Ah! Bach, Beethoven and Mozart were the favourites of the Free French. We also studied, rode horseback (Neptune knows why sailors always have to ride horses) took trips on bicycles to neighbouring parts and visited hotels on the other side of the river. The times of enforced leisure, when we were not passing time learning about engines and radar, made for very long days.

Then we slept on an opal sea, the sound of the engines silenced in the middle of the channel. Then might begin the pursuit and the chase, or we might be en route for a rendezvous ignored by the enemy. Quite often a convoy guarded the transport of troops, material for munitions. We would receive important signals about the route and speed. Night has fallen: we are on watch; we get back on the route; there is darkness and uncertainty; we approach the coast and can hear the noises of the countryside and smell the wood smoke - France!

Suddenly in a whisper, the voice of the Captain bending low over the men - "Enemy at 800m to starboard". End of the watch, end of the silence! End of the night, with a roar of engines, tremendously strong, firing and explosions our torpedo found its mark in the enemy shipping passing by. On our return the sun was already bathing the Devon coast and casting a touch of gold on the hair of our constant Wrens! It was a time of youth, of hope and of war. But where are the waves of yesterday? The Free French mixed well with local people and were popular, some even married local girls.

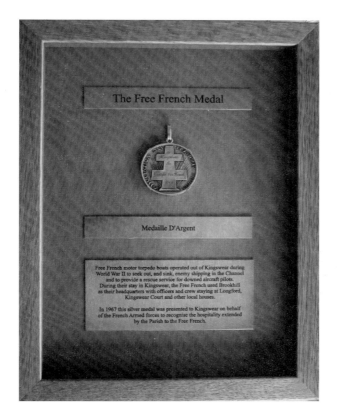

The Free French Medal

Medaille D'Argent

Free French motor torpedo boats operated out of Kingswear during
World War II to seek out, and sink, enemy shipping in the Channel
and to provide a rescue service for downed aircraft pilots.
During their stay in Kingswear, the Free French used Brookhill
as their headquarters with officers and crew staying at Longford,
Kingswear Court and other local houses.

In 1967 this silver medal was presented to Kingswear on behalf
of the French Armed forces to recognise the hospitality extended
by the Parish to the Free French.

The Free French Medal displayed in the Sarah Roope Trust Rooms acts as a fitting tribute to all those who were involved in such dangerous escapades.

This chapter would not be complete without mention of Captain Leon Coquerel. He was the tug boat captain originally based in Le Havre and took the opportunity in 1940 to escape the invading Germans and with the two tugs L'Isere and L'Aube arrived in Kingswear. He was based here for much of the rest of the war. The tugs were often seen moored alongside Belfort a French supply ship, yet remained very active in harbour duties working with Dart Harbour Navigation, as well as working with the Royal Navy, US Navy and Free French Forces.

Reg and Sheila Little remained friends with him after the war and Reg was asked to offer a eulogy to Leon at his funeral. I quote from part of his speech:

'Leon arrived as Captain of the tug boat 'Aube' in 1940 with many other "Free French" personnel. Leon took his new home to his heart - he made the acquaintance of many local residents including Ted and Doris Willing (Sheila Little's parents) who kept the Bar in the Royal Dart Hotel. As Doris spoke some

French, many of the newcomers spent a great deal time in the Hotel chatting with friends.

Leon became acquainted with Gertrude Perring and after the war they married and lived in France. They returned to Dartmouth regularly so that both could keep in touch with family and friends. We sometimes saw Leon on his return visits every August for the Dartmouth Regatta and he always sought us out! When his wife Gertrude died in 1994, he returned with her ashes to place them in the River Dart, which they both loved so much.'

Leon was kept busy on the Dart, but his skills as an experienced Captain were truly tested in 1942.

The following description comes from Don Collinson's book *Shipwrecks and Disasters on the River Dart:*

'While being towed by a trawler from Brixham to Fowey, a large J-Class yacht with only a Brixham deckhand Thomas Bray on board, encountered furious storms when only eleven miles out; this made the yacht unmanageable. They turned to seek the shelter of Dartmouth harbour, but in the entrance the tow parted. The trawler managed to pull alongside and another rope was thrown to Mr Bray who secured it to the towing post. Unfortunately the post broke. With great difficulty another rope was hurled aboard and this was secured to the winch, but this also broke away. By now things were critical and their plight was seen by Captain Leon Coquerel, Commander of the Dartmouth-based Aube. He steamed out and succeeded in drawing close enough for two of his crew members to scramble on board the yacht.

By now the seas were mountainous and they were unable to reach Mr Bray, who sadly was washed overboard from the stern and drowned. The yacht quickly began to sink so the two tugboat crewmen jumped overboard, one managing to swim to the safety of the tug but the other, when some twenty yards away, began to drown. Captain Coquerel bravely jumped overboard into the raging sea and with great difficulty secured the man until a launch arrived and hauled Captain Coquerel and the unconscious seaman aboard.

The town and the council were so impressed by this act of 'entente-cordiale gallantry' that the Mayor awarded to Captain Coquerel the Royal Humane Society bronze medal, bar, and certificate, at a civic gathering in the Guildhall.'

After his death in 1998 at the age of 97, Leon's ashes were also brought to be scattered near those of Gertrude. Leon decided that his medals should be given to Kingswear, a place that had captured his heart and benefitted from his presence.

Leon is seen here on his boat Aube, predictably wearing a beret; you can imagine that he would have worn the lapel badge of the Cross of Lorraine, top right, with enormous pride.

The top row of medals shows the French Merchant Marine medal; French Volunteer of the Resistance; London Medal for Saving Life at Sea

The middle row shows the Medal for Voluntary Service in Free France; French Resistance War Medal; 1939-1945 War Commemorative Medal; French Liberation Medal. This last medal depicts a map of France surrounded by a chain that is broken by two shellbursts, one in the northwest, the other in the southeast, i.e. one for each Allied landing place

The bottom row includes the British War Medal; British North West Europe Campaign Medal; British Victory Medal.

This is a presentation that is truly fitting of a remarkable man.

References:
Tony Higgins - The Free French in Kingswear – Dartmouth History Research Group
Reg Little – Growing up in Wartime Kingswear

10. Air raids and bombings

Although a number of air raids were aimed at both Dartmouth and Kingswear during the war, the lethal attack on the Philip and Son Shipyard at Noss had an enormous impact on the village of Kingswear. This chapter is largely devoted to the stories and memories of those whose lives were influenced by this episode.

Nova Varney was at home in bed with measles when Britannia Royal Naval College and Noss were bombed at 1130 on 18 September 1942. She never heard the explosions of the bombs but was deafened so much by the roar of the planes overhead heading for their targets, that she fell out of bed!

The War Records of 18 September 1942 note that 'at 1130 six Focke-Wulf 190s appeared at low level over Dartmouth. Bombs were dropped on shipbuilding works causing some damage and a number of casualties. Damage was also caused to The Royal Naval College and a collier was also sunk in the harbour. The enemy aircraft also machine gunned the area. Spitfires sighted four of these enemy aircraft, attacking three without visible results'. This report, probably quite deliberately, describes very little of what actually happened to Noss and the effect on the village.

A newspaper cutting at that time quotes 'a weather-beaten seaman' who described the action: 'Six enemy planes came in from the east'ard like a flock of gulls' he was quoted, 'skimming the surface of the sea so low that had a man been able to stand on the water his hat would have been knocked off his head. As they were just about 400 yards from the cliff they went in the air so straight you could see the whole top of each plane, and they went up three hundred feet. Then over they tipped to port and swooped down. A second or two later we heard explosions and saw clouds of smoke.' Another skipper described how close the planes were to his boat 'that I thought he would take the mast. He was only a few feet above the sea and we expected to see the mainsail in ribbons. It shook the mainsail so violently that it chucked it from the leeward to the windward.'

It seems that of the six attacking Focke-Wulf planes, the first two headed for Britannia Royal Naval College which was machine gunned and struck by two bombs. One Wren Petty Officer was killed and another officer injured. Fortunately the cadets were not in residence at the time or the casualties would have been much more severe. The next two planes aimed for the coal ships in the river. The Fernwood and a coal hulk Dagny were sunk, as was a crane. Fourteen were killed and several men ended up in the river. A Wren commandeered a launch and was able to rescue these cold, soaking frightened men from the water.

Two planes then headed onto the Philip Shipyard at Noss. They targeted the yard with landmines and bombs, as well as machine gun and cannon fire. The yard was badly damaged in the raid which killed fourteen men and three women immediately with another three workers dying of their wounds. Another forty people were injured but survived with treatment.

Damage to the machinery was considerable but the rest of the staff were determined to be back working, in whatever way they could, the next day. Eventually and after much effort, the works was back to full activity. At that time Philip and Son employed nearly 500 people at Noss with another 300 on the opposite bank of the River Dart at Sandquay. The General Manager, Mr Stewart, received an OBE in December 1942 for his effort. The Managing Director's Assistant, Mr McClarence, gained his OBE in the 1943 New Year's Honours List.

Frank Little worked at Noss and would cycle along the path from Kingswear alongside the railway track to and from work. The air raid took him totally by surprise; he remembers no siren or other warning, but thought that the planes came down the valley from Hillhead. The general level of noise in the workshop meant that he heard nothing until the sound of the wall behind him crashing

down. He was understandably terrified. His brother Bert was amongst the twenty killed. Immediately Frank asked the other workers if his brother was OK, their eyes did not meet his, but they just looked away. Bert had been killed instantly. He remembers being back at work the next day - 'you just have to get on with it' he was told. Sheila Little reflects on the attitude then of support and sympathy, but with a 'chin up and look on the bright side' approach compared with the 'touchy-feely' and counselling response that might be expected now.

The Little family lived at 1 Agra Villas at that time and were overwhelmed by letters of sympathy. Reg and Frank have been exceedingly generous in allowing me to see the large file of these letters which have remained private for almost 70 years. The letters came from every corner of Kingswear and many from further afield.

George Herbert Frank Little, seen above as a young boy, had spent some time at school in Dartmouth. The headmaster wrote 'it seems only the other day that Herbert was with us at school. He was such a promising lad and I am sure would have done well had God seen fit to spare him'. Mrs E Melville of Kingswear Lodge remembered him from the First Aid lectures in the village hall and extended her sympathy to the whole family. The Commanding Officer of Dartmouth Air Cadets Force, W Harris, wrote to Cadet Reg Little extending the company's sincere sympathy and continuing: 'may the One Above comfort and sustain you and yours in this dark hour and grant that you will all meet again some day'.

Lionel Fairweather was Chairman of the Parish Council as well as in charge of the ARP section. He wrote to extend the 'deepest sympathy from the ARP personnel in the sad loss of your son' who had 'been held in the highest esteem by all in this Parish'.

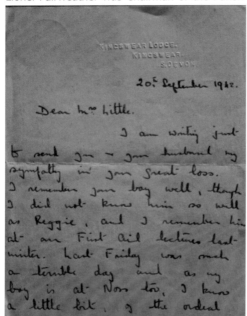

Telegrams also arrived in considerable numbers. The sender would go to their nearest Post Office to buy a telegram which was a very succinct message. This was charged by the number of words chosen. The message was telegraphed to the Post Office at the receiving end where the words were written onto a form. This was then speedily delivered to the recipient.

The Kingswear Post Office was run by Samuel Wellington and was next door to Charlie Heal's sweet shop cum barber. Charlie Heal was also the Postman and if you were half way through your haircut when an urgent telegram came through, you had to wait for the finishing snip until the telegram had been delivered! Perhaps this telegram dated 23 September was written by Charlie Heal himself before being delivered to the grieving Little family. That day was a Wednesday and Bert's funeral

took place in Kingswear Cemetery at 3.30 that afternoon.

In Loving Remembrance of

George Herbert Frank Little

Aged 17 years.

Killed by Enemy Action 18th September, 1942.

Buried in Kingswear Cemetery, Devon.
September 23rd, 1942.

Although he was only 17, Bert was a member of the National Fire Service, Kingswear Church Choir and Kingswear Boy Scouts. His coffin was 'covered with a wealth of flowers and brought to the church on the fire engine manned by his mates and preceded by the Scouts'.

In Memory
— of —

THE MEN AND WOMEN WHO LOST THEIR LIVES BY ENEMY ACTION AT NOSS SHIPYARD. SEPTEMBER 18TH 1942.

FREDERICK. C. ADAMS.	HENRY. J. LUCKHURST.
JOHN. R. ASH.	JOHN. MARTIN.
DAVID BOTT.	SIDNEY. POPE.
JOHN. G .C. BUSTIN.	ERNEST. POOLE.
ROSE. A. CRANG.	HUBERT. E.W. PUTT.
THOMAS. FARR.	EWART. E. TRANT.
RICHARD. FRANKLIN.	NELLIE. E .TREBILCOCK.
LIONEL. E. HOLDEN.	SAMUEL. J. VEALE.
WALTON. LEWIS	FREDERICK. VICKERY.
GEORGE .H. F. LITTLE.	HAZEL. J. WEAVER.

Rev Keyworth later took a Service of Remembrance at Noss when, after prayers, the congregation sang 'O God our help in ages past' before the Memorial tablet was unveiled. This was removed from the Noss Shipyard to Kingswear Church when the yard closed down.

Maurice Ashton remembers many local wartime events. At the age of 14 he was working as a courier at the Noss shipyard of Philip and Son. The day of the bombing remains vividly and emotionally in his mind. There was no warning of the air raid but just the most colossal explosion and noise he had ever heard. He was immediately aware of considerable devastation around him. Mr Sim, the workshop manager, rapidly assessed the situation and asked Maurice to get back home and gather as many sheets as possible to tear up into bandages. Perhaps it was also a way of removing the teenager from the horrific scene for a period of time. Maurice raced back along the railway track as fast as he could. When he returned to the yard, the survivors of the blast were gathered outside for a roll call. Maurice's return was greeted with joy. They had assumed that his absence suggested that he was amongst the casualties. Mr Sim's instruction to get the sheets had not filtered through with the inevitable concern for Maurice's safety.

Sheila Little would travel to and from school in Totnes by train from Kingswear station. When they left school that day, they had heard nothing of the lethal attacks on the river and Noss. The railway line escaped punishment from the bombers and the return train trundled past the devastated site as usual. Sheila was horrified to see people covered with oil and dirt trying to search the rubble of the shipyard.

A newspaper cutting, describing only a 'SW coastal town', highlights the praise for the emergency services with the 'Police and Special Constables were at once on duty and rendered every possible help. The greatest praise has been given on all sides to the Ambulance Service, Red Cross nurses and doctors who worked under extreme pressure all day and performed magnificent service. Flags were flown at half mast in the town.

In October 1988 The Herald Express published this photograph. In recognition of the 20 people who died as a result of that raid, a Commemorative Stone was sited with a cast iron cannon at the Sandquay site of Philip and Son. A blessing was given by Rev John Butler. Mr Ken Wills, the managing director, was also present. George Causey who was hit by 14 machine gun bullets and shrapnel amazingly survived but was blinded by his injuries, is seen with his guide dog Williams.

The wording on the stone tablet reads:

'DEDICATED TO THE MEMORY OF THE TWENTY MEN AND WOMEN WHO LOST THEIR LIVES BY ENEMY ACTION AT PHILIP AND SONS NOSS SHIPYARD ON 18TH SEPTEMBER 1942

The memorial stone was moved from the Sandquay site when that area was redeveloped. The stone was returned to the Noss yard in 2010 with a further service of dedication at that time.

18 September 1942 was a memorable day for another villager, Dennis Thyer. Billy Peters was a local fisherman whose motor boat was moored in the middle of the river. As he had a bad heart he encouraged local lads to row him from

Kingswear out to the mooring. Both Dennis Thyer and Reg Little often helped him. On the day in question Dennis was asked by Billy to take the rowing boat across to Dartmouth. A large drum of diesel was gently lowered from the embankment into the back of the boat. This left the boat rather stern heavy, so Dennis moved as far forward as possible to level the boat. Nevertheless progress was rather slow and as he reached mid river he saw German planes flying over to bomb Noss, sinking the two colliers as they went. As they returned down the river they had their machine guns blazing, aiming for the naval vessels moored mid stream. He was by now almost alongside one such vessel and a sailor on board yelled at him to get closer to seek some shelter from the gunfire. On the basis that the ship was the target he was not convinced of this plan! Dennis happily escaped the scene unscathed but with lifelong memories of a very scary morning.

During the hostilities Marjorie Reeves remembers a bomb falling through the roof of Kingston Farm barns, and another into the field between Coleton Barton Farm and Kingston Farm. This landed just as a driver was making a delivery to Brownstone Farm. The petrified man appeared at their front door, seeking refuge, covered in earth but unharmed! She told me that 'We did have a Spitfire crash on the farm one day; luckily, the pilot escaped, bailed out; we were all very excited and went out to have a look, but it was guarded night and day. I can't remember how they ever got it away. By now the RAF Kingswear camp was fully manned and we had the Commanding Officer billeted with us. Then a little while later the Women's Auxiliary Air Force Officer, Miss Spool, came and lived with us at home. The WAAFs and the RAF boys that were on the camp were billeted around various farms and in Brixham with a transport lorry taking them backwards and forwards for the different shifts. They called each day for milk from the farm. There was no canteen at the Radar site; they just made cups of tea or coffee'.

Marjorie also remembers a German plane crash landing into one of their fields. Quite possibly during the same raid, Mr Thomas, Marjorie's father and tenant of Coleton farm, was threshing corn in one of the fields adjacent to the Radar installation.

Mr Yeomans, his rick maker, was helping him with hayfork in his hand. They were startled by the noise of the low flying aircraft coming over the sea and then swooping up over the installation. As the plane roared overhead Mr Yeomans was heard to say 'if I had put my fork up I could have touched the bloody thing!'

Dick Harris recalled that the unexploded bomb was scrutinised by one of the farm hands, who offered to put a rope around it and tow it elsewhere with a recently acquired tractor! Nina Hannaford recalls that this was her uncle, John Hannaford, who worked with Mr Coaker of Kingston Farm. It was he who had the cunning idea of towing the bomb away! At that moment, and probably very fortunately, the ARP and Bomb Disposal squads were soon in attendance and took safe control of the situation! The characters of *Dad's Army* come flooding to mind!

Dick also remembered the terror of low flying enemy aircraft. During sorties over the Dart the planes would fire tracer rounds which would skim over his head! One shell in ten was a tracer, the rest were live rounds. Not only did these terrify him but they would also terrify his horses. He would need to stay on his feet to hold the horses under some sort of control. If he had been on his own, he would have fallen to the ground for safety very rapidly!

COTTAGES HIT BY BOMB

Woman Extricated From Debris

There was another raid on 27 November 1940. Reg Little says that the first of two bombs to drop in the locality was in Wilful Murder Field, causing no damage. As you drive into the village from the cemetery, past Castella on your right, there is a left hand bend then Sunny Cottage before the right hand bend. Wilful Murder Field is on the left.

Jack Eveleigh lived in Sunny Cottage but was working at the station when that bomb dropped. He raced home to see what the damage was and was greatly relieved to find very minor damage to the cottage and only a small amount of plaster off his bedroom ceiling. If the pilot had dropped the bombs moments later the devastation of Kingswear would really have been 'wilful murder'!

The second bomb dropped on the two cottages at the entrance to Hoodown Farm Lane, completely demolishing them. The lady from one cottage was taken to Brixham Hospital and her wounds dressed. The next day, a taxi from Higher Garage (Couch & Stoneman) driven by Roy Kelland was sent to the hospital to take the lady to her temporary home. This was to be the Old Cricket Pavilion near Fountain Violet Farm. Roy was told to take her via Nethway, so that she couldn't see the ruins of her old home. Apparently she made Roy stop and take her past the ruins, where she used very strong language about Hitler!

A newspaper cutting of 28 November describes the events in greater detail:
'Fred Jane and his wife Violet had a miraculous escape from death when an enemy aircraft dropped two bombs close to each other yesterday afternoon. The first bomb destroyed two cottages and cratered the lane. The demolition was so complete that rafters, masonry and household effects were reduced to a

mass of debris. Mrs Jane was completely buried. Her husband heard her groans, located her and rushed with other helpers, to extricate her from the mass of rubble. She was then taken to hospital.' At this point Nurse Sandy appeared on the scene. 'I was in a car with a patient and his wife when two bombs dropped about 20 or 30 yards away. The car which was parked at the side of the road was rocked by the explosion which destroyed the two cottages' she said. 'The other bomb felled a tree which was thrown across the road blocking it for traffic. Mr Jane pointed to a heap of rubble and indicated that his wife was underneath. It seemed incredible that anyone buried under all that rubble could have escaped death.'

She was extricated under the direction of a doctor. 'She was buried in an upright position with a terrible head injury. The work of getting her out could not be hurried.' Mrs Jane suffered a fractured arm, lacerations to her head, bruising to her body and shock. Mr Jane said that he was on a half day off from work and had been in the garden. Mrs Jane had come to the door and was discussing having a cup of tea when the bomb dropped close to them.

Mr Jane remembered falling to the floor and covering his face with his hands. He then looked round after the second bomb dropped to see that the cottage had been demolished. He then discovered his buried wife but was relieved to hear her breathing. Mr Coaker from Kingston Farm was driving by and stopped to help, together with Nurse Sandy.

Reg Little recalls waiting in The Square and seeing a large plane flying up and down the river. Soon a Spitfire came along 'and had several goes at it'. It then flew below the German plane, which was photographing the harbour, and got shot down by the belly turret.

The Spitfire crashed into the sea by Eastern Blackstone after the pilot had baled out. He was picked up safely and the engine trawled up in the 1970s! This photograph of a painting came from Don Collinson and shows the tussle between the Spitfire and Dornier over the river. Its origin is unknown.

Another raid saw a bomb drop on Church Hill behind the garage of The Chalet, remembers Jack Eveleigh. The explosion was such that the car was catapulted out of the garage, across the road and was embedded in the front wall of The Keep, the house on the opposite side of the road! The bomb crater became a piece of creative landscaping and converted into a sunken garden! Sheila Little was afflicted by German measles on that day and was in bed at home, Alta Vista, now Prospect House, at the top of Church Hill. As the planes flew low overhead their roar and the explosions of the bombs startled her considerably.

Another episode had Jack Eveleigh chuckling as he recounted the tale to me. A bomb had fallen on Castle Road towards Brookhill. Sam Hawke and another Home Guard were responsible for overseeing the area until the bomb disposal squad arrived. They roped off the road and ensured that no-one gained access to the area. It was night and they fell asleep. When they woke the following morning they discussed the situation:

'The bomb disposal squad will be here soon' said one.
'Yes shouldn't be too long now' replied the other.
At that moment Sam looked up to the clear morning sky. 'Was there a gale last night?'
'No.'
Well why is that large branch broken?' as they looked up to the tree above them.
'Let's have a closer look.'
And they did to reveal the branch on the ground adjacent to them and the tail fin of a second unexploded bomb half hidden just feet from where they lay all night!

Reg Little was involved in the aftermath of one of the bombing raids; 'one Saturday morning in 1943 at about 11 am, I was in Lower Contour Road, planes approached and several explosions ensued. Being in the First Aid Party at the time although only aged 15, I went down to Mr Fairweather's garage where we kept a Commer Brake ambulance with two stretchers, which we had recently been allocated. Mr Charles Bovey was in charge of the First Aid Party. We went immediately to Dartmouth where the bombs had fallen on the Town Arms and the Bank in Duke Street. We were directed to the Duke Street incident and were involved in digging out bodies, helping injured people and retrieving some of the money in buckets. We were involved there on the Saturday and Sunday until about 7pm. On the Sunday the last bodies were dug out of the Bank. In those days there was no "trauma counselling" for 15 year olds. If you were working as an adult you were expected to behave like one.'

Margaret Rickard was working in the Post Office in Dartmouth during both the town bombing and the Noss attacks. As a Red Cross nurse she rushed to Dartmouth Hospital to help with both incidents. After the Noss raid she described many walking wounded arriving at the hospital as well as many severely injured workers, some of whom required months of hospital treatment. She was hardly aware of the aircraft coming in for the Dartmouth raid, but heard 'the most tremendous explosion' as the bombs dropped on the Butterwalk area. Pat Henshall had gained her Red Cross Certificate while in the Girl Guides. She also worked in Boots at the time of the raids where they ran a first aid post. After the bombing she was summoned for her bandaging skills! She also recalls watching the planes fly over to bomb Plymouth and the bright orange glow in the sky as the city burned.

Many of the locals remembered that German planes had been seen making

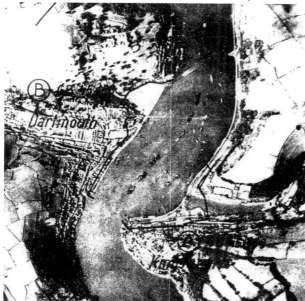

reconnaissance flights over the Dart in order to plan their raids. Don Collinson was able to acquire this aerial photograph of the area.

This example of a German aerial reconnaissance photograph shows Kingswear in the bottom right hand corner, with Dartmouth in the middle of the photograph. The Higher Ferry appears to be on the Dartmouth slipway with a number of boats moored in the river. The date of this photograph is 21 November 1939.

Late in 1940, the Littles recall, a Norwegian tanker arrived in the estuary for an overnight stop. It had steamed from the Gulf and had been attacked and bombed several times en route. It was probably seeking some shelter and rest and perhaps taking the opportunity of coaling from one of the coalers moored in the river. The following morning she left the river but was bombed and sunk off Mansands. The bow was visible for several days and oil spilled onto the beach. The crew are buried in Brixham Cemetery.

References:
Philip and Son Ltd Shipbuilders & Engineers by Derek Blackhurst
The Herald Express
I am especially grateful to the Little family for sight of their personal records

11. The Scouts, School and Evacuees

The majority of 'the locals' I have been able to talk to were, of course, children during the war. Most memories of Kingswear School are very positive and the influence of the teaching they received remains with most of the pupils. Some had already reached their teenage years by 1939 and some did so before 1945. For most of them the war years were not distressing times but produced a sense of excitement and adventure. There were some very clear exceptions, however, which are to be found elsewhere in this book. This chapter will start with the Scout group that was thriving at the time.

The Scouts

Reg Little reflects on his childhood days in 'Growing up in wartime Kingswear':
'When War broke out I was a member of Kingswear Scouts and aged 12. Our first task was to meet the evacuees, who arrived by train from London (Acton) and to take them to their billets, the homes they would be staying in. A section of the local Red Cross, under Mrs. Melville of Kingswear House, Beacon Road and Mrs Tabb, the village midwife, who lived in Cemetery Lodge dealt with the arrival of the evacuees.'

'After the long journey some of the evacuees were frightened and upset and all were worn out. However, they were made a fuss of, given good meals and put to bed. Kingswear School suddenly increased in size. The classes were doubled and there were extra teachers under Miss Heywood, the Head. All was quiet for the next twelve months of the "phoney" war and quite a few of the evacuees returned to their homes. Various large houses in Kingswear were requisitioned, including The Priory, The Beacon, Inverdart, The Mount, Mount Ridley, Brookhill, Kingswear Court, Nethway House and the Redoubt (now Kingswear Park).'

'Our Scout Headquarters had been given to us in 1936 by Colonel Davies. His wife was a member of the Wills Tobacco Company. With great publicity the hut was unceremoniously taken back from us and in its place twelve months later a static water tank was built. It was thought locally that Colonel Davies had hoped for a Knighthood for the gift of the Scout Hut and, when he didn't receive one, he took the hut back! Our Scoutmaster had been called up, he was a Captain in the Territorial Army and there were no Scouters left to protest about the hut. We lost the best Scout HQ in the West. It had been complete with a collapsible boxing ring, parallel bars, climbing ropes, a vaulting horse, and it included a large hall and other rooms. It was situated in the quarry where Mount Pleasant Flats now stand. Our next Scout HQ was kindly lent to us by Mr Jack Tribble a builder. It had been the Men's Club before the Kingswear Hall was built. It was above the workshop in an old warehouse in Brixham Road, where the flats opposite the entrance to the Marina Car Park now stand.'

'The twenty four Scouts in our group collected paper, cardboard, newspaper and all types of metal every Saturday all through the War. It was stacked in the garage next to the Ship Inn. The Rural District Council collected it and sold it, but the Scouts never received a penny of the proceeds from The Rural District Council!'

Reg continues 'In 1941 I was the oldest Scout and the Troop Leader; we went to Galmpton by train for a summer camp. The land belonged to Hugh Goodeson who was in charge of the local civil defence. For that camp we had about thirty scouts, some of whom were evacuees. We also had several long weekend camps. Would parents now allow someone aged 14 to take their children away like that?' (No, Reg, I suspect you are right!) 'Those of us who are left have happy memories', he continues.

'The planes heading for Plymouth would fly overhead and the nearby gun emplacements would open fire. You were not allowed to camp within a mile of the guns, but guns could fire towards you! We remember being unable to wake Douglas Roper one night during a raid, he still complains we interrupted his sleep! We were camping there on the Sunday that St Marychurch Sunday School in Torquay was bombed killing many children.' That was on Sunday 30 May 1943 and Eileen Sumner recounts the story of her being rescued from the rubble in 'Memories of Life during World War II' by the Babbacombe & St Marychurch Local History Group.

Reg continues 'When the Americans arrived with their landing craft, they moored in Galmpton. Quite a number of the troops who had been Scouts in America came to visit us and for sometime after we had ample supplies of food and chocolate!'

'Village children used to play in Mr Roberts' part of Hoodown Woods all day. Parents felt quite safe about allowing their children to play out all day in those days. The children liked to scramble after bombs had dropped to see who could collect the most shrapnel. On Saturdays the Scouts used to go to the butcher's shop and buy sausages, which weren't rationed, and cook them with chips on fires made from old cans with holes knocked in them, in which we burnt coal picked up between the railway lines. We also made rafts on which we sailed the creek. Sometimes we fell in, of course, and had to dry our clothes while we were cooking. Our rafts were based at Brewhouse Beach in the Creek. This land belonged to the Parish and if the Station Master kept us off the sidings, Brewhouse was our retreat. On the whole Mr Bovey, the stationmaster, was very good to us.'

When I was aged 13, I used to go out crabbing with Bill Peters on Saturdays and during the school holidays on his "crabbie" (crab boat) the DH80, which had a petrol engine. He lived in the Mill House at the end of Kingswear Creek. He was the person who had the house converted in about 1938. We used to go up as far as Mansands and Eastern Blackstone and as far down as Strete and Blackpool. We used to get quite a few crabs and lobsters. I remember that he once put in an illegal salmon net in Robin Hood's Cove. He wanted me to work with him when I left school, but my father wanted me to have a trade. One evening, when going to the moorings, we saw a body floating by. It was taken in tow by a Naval Picket boat. It was a Norwegian Seaman who had fallen overboard at Sandquay and had been lodged under the floating dock for some three weeks. Phew!'

At times the boys of Kingswear would help on the railway and a favourite task was to work the turntable. Terry Satchell was on the footplate with the driver when German planes roared low over the river. With a firm push and encouragement from the driver, he was sheltering under the train faster than he could think! Were the planes heading for Britannia Royal Naval College that day?

The School

Mike Short remembers that gas masks were issued to everyone. Fred Eckhart of 2 Jubilee Terrace, who was probably in the ARP or Home Guard to have such a job, arrived with another man to fit the masks. Children had to take the masks with them to school each day and this was checked by the teachers. What was the discipline from Miss Heywood for those who forgot?

Mike Short also remembers that school games would always have been outside rather than indoors, and attributes his good health to this. He was also aware that cases of scarlet fever, diphtheria, mumps, measles and scabies were not unusual and that one family was home for almost six months with scabies! Childhood immunisations and antibiotics were still some way off!

Gillian Bovey recalls that Brian thought that Miss Heywood was firm, but usually fair. She then retold Brian's story that he was kept in detention every afternoon for one week and caned each day. This was apparently for throwing a stone through the school window which he always denied! He went to a Torquay school after leaving Kingswear School.

Nova Varney started school at 4½ and learnt to add up on an abacus with Miss Lawrie, who also taught her needlework. Nova was 'often sent out of the classroom for talking'. The punishment was to stand in the school hallway for the prescribed amount of time. However, the store cupboard was also in the hallway and not usually locked. Despite rationing there was always a tin of drinking chocolate powder lying in wait on the shelf. A lick of the finger, a dip into the tub and then a finger suck was inevitable...... and very easy to repeat again and again! How worthwhile was it to be in disgrace in the hallway? Nevertheless she was never caned unlike her cousin Margaret Fabian who was 'always being caned' and described Nova as 'goody-two-shoes'.

Miss Heywood was 'a marvellous lady' who organised memorable nature walks. 'She gave me my love of nature', which Nova still cherishes, especially when doing her watercolour painting. Miss Heywood also impressed on Nova the essence of good handwriting using a fountain pen and the way the pen strokes should be made – 'up thin, down thick'

Margaret Fabian's school days would consist of walking to school along Castle Road each morning and evening. The soldiers guarding the lane would call out 'stop, who goes there' ensuring that they were bone fide before allowing them to continue on their way. This was clearly an important part of security but no doubt quite scary for a young child after dusk in the blackout. Miss Heywood, the head teacher, was 'very fond of caning' and a real disciplinarian but a good teacher well respected and fondly remembered. Kingswear School would take children in the 5-11 range, after that they would go to Dartmouth School.

Terry Satchell also went to Kingswear School under the headship of Miss Heywood who he felt was firm but fair most of the time. He also thought she was a little enthusiastic with the cane. He remembers that he and George Radford were playing piggy back in the playground. Mary Scoble, the butcher's daughter, interpreted this as a fight and reported them to Miss Heywood. Six of the best in her office was Miss Heywood's plan. The boys had to bend over the cast iron fire surround to receive their punishment. Apparently Miss Heywood's eyesight was poor as was her aim! Terry remembers more canes being broken on the fire surround than landed on his backside! During his days at Kingswear School he remembers the drill of an air raid with the firm instruction to seek shelter, either in the proper air raid shelter just below the school or under the table. Not for Terry though, he felt it was much more fun to stay by the window and offer a running commentary on what the planes were up to!

Miss Heywood would teach swimming in school playground, describing the breast stroke sequence with 1-2-3 and arm movements. When she thought you were good enough it was off to Lighthouse Beach for the real thing! Who thought the water was cold? She also taught Margaret Fabian and her peers sewing and knitting, even making woollen socks that were 'never the same size or shape' for airmen. 'She taught us everything we learnt' reflected Margaret.

A dentist would occasionally call at the school. Margaret remembers him passing his instruments through a Bunsen burner before use and would pull out teeth there and then if needed! May Crisp was Margaret's best friend at that time and they continue to correspond even though May now lives in Australia.

Daily routines at school would include taking your own gas mask in case of attack and the obligatory, love it or hate it, 1/3 pint of milk daily! One privilege was to be chosen as straw monitor. That pupil would be in charge of handing out straws for the milk, while the ink monitor would wash the ink wells and top them up with fresh ink. This was made up from powder and mixed with water. Those were the days of old type pens and nibs that required frequent dipping into the ink well!

Pat Henshall describes herself as being very shy at school, although she was rapped over the knuckles for a now forgotten misdemeanour during sewing! It was during these lessons that she learned the 'make do and mend' motto to which she still subscribes. She also felt that Miss Heywood was very much in charge at the school and you certainly did what she said! Pat thinks she was probably in her 50s, never married and lived in one of the cottages on Brixham Road. She was respected in the village as a good teacher but did not seem to socialise very much.

The Evacuees

Evacuated children were taught in a separate part of the school from the local children. Even three days before the declaration of war on 3 September 1939 the evacuation of children and adults had begun. They would be moved from high risk areas. Sometimes mothers would accompany the children, but often the youngsters would travel without their parents. By the end of that month almost two million people had been moved, mainly from the London area. Early in 1940 more than one hundred mothers and their children arrived by train in Kingswear. Boys from a Dartmouth school came across the river to help the arrival of these Londoners. Tired, hungry and probably very frightened they were placed with local families to start their new lives. A sticker could be placed in the window to show that the occupants were part of the Evacuation Scheme, and evacuees had been taken in.

Edna Knapman was evacuated from London together with her brothers and two of her sisters. They had never been on a train before and never been beyond the city. She recalls that she was placed with her two sisters in the home of Mr & Mrs Bartlett. He was a retired fisherman. At school they were referred to as the 'Lifebuoy kids' as they were always washed by Mrs Bartlett in that soap!

Their family home in Camberwell had been bombed three times. Her father was away in the RAF but her mother and her eldest sister, now aged 14, continued working in London as they were considered safe. It was eighteen months later that she saw her mother again when she was relocated to Brixham. Initially she was able to take her sons into her new home, and then a while later the girls left the care of Mr and Mrs Bartlett. Eventually her father was demobbed to Brixham as well.

Edna also remembers that Mrs Bartlett would invite the boys for Sunday tea every week. 'We were never short of anything' she reflects. There was always a cooked breakfast of bacon, eggs and fried white pudding, or 'hog's pudding' and fried potatoes 'like I've never been able to do myself'.

When Plymouth was being bombed so extensively planes could be seen flying overhead at night heading for the city. One of the Plymouth Children's Homes was evacuated to Nethway House. Sheila Little, as a First Aider, would go to Nethway House to practice lowering children out of the windows in case of attack.

Mike Short wrote 'Thinking and talking about the evacuees I was at school with, it's strange how some are remembered by many and some not at all. The Dudley twins, Maurice and Alan (of The Creek Incident fame) are remembered by many but the other three brothers John, Trevor and Roger hardly recalled. John went almost at once to Dartmouth Grammar School so he must have taken and passed the exam when he lived in Islington, from where they were evacuated. They all lived at 1 Alma Place with a Mrs. Richardson. This ties in with their relationship with Terry Satchell who now lives in Paignton, and his mother's maiden name was Richardson. The family had trawlers in Brixham. Did I mention Roy and Sylvia Springham?' Mike continues: 'Roy is dead but Sylvia has given me permission to tell her story. They were billeted with Mr and Mrs Maurice Weller and at the end of the war their father came, as Sylvia thought, to take them both home, but he would only take Roy as he was about to leave school, I don't know of their mother. Sylvia stayed and was adopted by the Wellers. She was very happy although her adopted father always said he really wanted a son. Mrs Weller died when Sylvia was twenty and about the time Sylvia got married. Sylvia's story tells of the disruption to family life the war caused.

Pat Henshall's parents looked after two sisters who were evacuated from London. Mildred, the younger girl, arrived with only the clothes she was wearing. Mrs Hall was soon over in Dartmouth with the young lass to find more clothes for her. These were acquired with the family ration tokens and supplemented by Mrs Hall's sewing skills.

Tony Read reflects on his wartime experiences in his article 'World War II and my part in it'.

He writes 'We were placed in one of a row of three storey houses at the end of Lower Contour Road. The far house was lived in by Frank and Granny Knapman who took us into their home and hearts, and it seemed as if we slept for the first time. Grandad Knapman was a porter on Kingswear station, Granny Knapman's family lived next door and I think their daughter was called Myra. They had three children. Monica was the eldest, then Lizzie and then Brian who got up to all sorts of mischief and always had grazed knees and torn trousers. At the far end lived the Beerman family. Mr Beerman drove the small ferry boat. Their daughter was called Brenda.

I only had one toy in the world, and it was a tattered wooden scooter that my dad made for me out of odd bits of wood. It worked wonders for my image and increased my esteem and popularity; the equivalent to owning an E-Type Jag for pulling the dollies.

Behind these houses lived the Pollard family. They were all boys older than me and they were my heroes. They knew all the things that needed knowing. Where the best trees to climb were, the nearest place to scrump apples and so on. They also did exciting things. Once they found a box of live .303 rifle ammunition. They drilled a hole through their gatepost that was a tight fit for the bullets and then put a six-inch nail against the end of the cartridge and hit it with a hammer. There was an almighty bang and the business end of the bullet whizzed and flew across the valley. They were always in trouble. They were my heroes, the Pollards.

My big brother, Pete, went to the Grammar School over at Dartmouth and I went to the junior school just up from the station. We had a very elegant lady teacher once called Miss Matt-Souki and we bad-mannered little horrors used to drive her mad by pretending we couldn't pronounce it and called her Miss Matooky. She hated us.

My father was sent to Ridley House after receiving injuries on his Motor Torpedo Boat. They used to sail from Falmouth and go across the channel to sort out the German ships, and then tear back home like scalded cats, and go straight down to the pub.

The steep gardens of the cottages led down to a road which we called Lower Road; its real name was Brixham Rd. We all used to scamper down there to a bungalow and ask Mrs Bunn if John could come out to play. We thought they must be pretty rich because it was rumoured that they had a car. Nobody had a car then.

One of my greatest delights was to have a ride on The Mew; that beautiful Great Western Railway steamer that was kept in permanent steam with the sole purpose of completing the last two hundred yards of the trip to Dartmouth for anyone who bought a rail ticket to that town. It must have cost a fortune to run, but for me it was paradise. I soon grovelled my way into the skipper's good books and was allowed below decks in the engine room to watch the magnificent triple-expansion, reciprocating steam engine come to life and almost silently push the ship gently across the river. In that engine room it was the first time that a little boy had shed tears of happiness for quite some time.

But me being a nasty little horror, I showed my gratitude by carving my name on the aftrail at the stern of the ship. Years later, when I heard that The Mew was in Demelweeks scrap yard waiting to be broken up, I headed there and pointed to my name and thus my shameful vandalism, bunged the man a tenner, and said, "Save me that piece." He nodded and pocketed the tenner. I think you know the end of the story....serves me right.

In the summer time we all used to go down to Lighthouse Beach (for beach read rocks) and although the water was almost always at minus 95 Centigrade we loved it. The very active sewage outfall pipe didn't seem to worry us (there was no `elf and safety' then) but we most likely picked up a hatful of immunities that saved our lives many times since. If we were off for the whole day it could mean a trip round to Millbay Beach and that had real sand. Cor heck!

More than once I saw aeroplanes flying down over the river, these were usually Spitfires identified by the heavenly sound of their Rolls Royce Merlin V12 engines. They might well have been chasing enemy planes, but I never saw any. That didn't stop me from telling my spellbound mates back home that the whole Battle of Britain was fought here – and I saw it all happen, so there!

Eventually our house had a new roof, walls, windows and doors and it was time to go home. For me being in Kingswear was a magical time and I lived among some wonderful people.

My brother Pete joined the RAF and died, with his crew, flying a Wellington Bomber in 1951. I joined the Merchant Navy and terrified the passengers on Union Castle liners before they threw me out. I often think of the Kingswear people and wonder how many are still around. They will always be alive in my memories'.

One Sunday Jim was asked to volunteer with other children and adults for an emergency exercise. A label describing his 'injuries' was attached and he had to lie in the middle of Fore Street until the medics arrived and eventually was taken away on a stretcher to the village hall.

Where the new marina is now, Motor Torpedo Boats and other small war launches would tie up to load stores and he would frequently go down to watch. Very often, when loading ammunition, some would fall over the side. He suspects that it was never retrieved and there must be a large amount still down there. There is another story of a bomb dropping in the mud somewhere in the vicinity of the footbridge. It did not explode but by the next morning it had sunk out of sight. Douglas Roper also recalls watching from his bedroom window an unexploded bomb drop in Waterhead Creek which similarly disappeared overnight.

Jim also remembers D Day and all the troops and ships sailing from Dartmouth. President Roosevelt had died and the ships were displaying their flags at half mast. His mother was asked after the war, when the Royal Navy ships were decommissioned, whether she could put on a bit of a spread and have a party upstairs in the Steam Packet. He remembers her saying that if they want some sandwiches then they must provide the fillings and the butter. A day later a 24 pound case of butter was in their kitchen!

The end of hostilities at last! As part of a village party local and evacuee children parade through The Square with banners and Union Flags. They are clearly enjoying themselves and have turned out in their best VE day outfits! Just visible is the bricked up archway to the left of Charlie Heal's shop, now the Post Office, which was part of one of the village air raid shelters. In the window above are the young faces of Margaret Heal and her sister Audrey!

Acknowledgements to Margaret Rickard, Beryl Drew, Mike Short and Tony Read
Dartmouth & Kingswear during the second world war – Arthur Clamp
Life at Kingswear School during the war – Michael Stevens

12. The Railway and Ferries

When Isambard Kingdom Brunel brought the first train into Kingswear in 1864, he could not possibly have imagined how, less than eighty years later, the same tracks would carry such a heavy responsibility. The importance of the railway to the war effort is hard to exaggerate. The keenly anticipated summer holiday of the 1930s, arriving by train from the Midlands or the Home Counties, came to a rapid halt. Timetables were revised to remove any service that was not absolutely necessary, thereby helping to save essential fuel.

At times during the war the river between Kingswear and Dartmouth, as well as upstream towards Noss, was heavily congested with boats. It has been said that you could almost walk from riverbank to riverbank across the decks of the moored boats. All of this fleet needed provisions, fuel, crew changes, munitions and general supplies so what better means of supply than from the railway system.

An extra jetty was built at Kingswear, adjacent to the Forwood siding, to allow the fleet of Motor Torpedo Boats to refuel more easily. Whilst this construction was underway in 1941 a lorry aiming to deliver supplies to the building site got stuck while crossing the railway lines at Hoodown. Unfortunately the next train from Churston was unable to stop and the truck driver was killed and thrown into the river.

In May 1942 the King and Queen visited Kingswear and Dartmouth. A special train was organised by Mr R H Bovey, the Kingswear Stationmaster. A naval launch then took them across the river to be greeted by the Mayor and Mayoress of Dartmouth. After meeting Officer Cadets and Wrens at Britannia Royal Naval Collge, they left Kingswear on a late train.

There had been a steady supply of Yorkshire coal from the northeast prior to the war, and this continued. A regular shuttle service of coalers, of the Everard fleet, would leave from Hull; they would sail down the east coast and into the Channel heading for the Dart. Eddie Smales who now lives in Kingswear, was born in Hull then evacuated to Hook near Goole. He worked on such a coal boat. The trip would take two days from Hull to Kingswear, two days to unload, then two days back to Hull where reloading would take another day. It was during these two unloading days that he met Maureen Stanleick and subsequently married her. During the war and at times of high risk to shipping in the Channel, domestic coal came via the west coast and Irish Sea.

Coal boats would tie up alongside the Kingswear quay and cranes with grabs would unload the coal from the boat into waiting train wagons. Most of the coal would be bound for the Torquay gas works. However 200 tons of each consignment would be taken over the river to the Dartmouth gas works situated by the North Embankment. The unloading of the coal was arranged by the then local coal merchants, Renwick, Wilton & Dobson Ltd.

As the boats came alongside between fifteen and twenty men, known as coal trimmers, climbed aboard. As the crane grabs emptied the hold, the job of the trimmers was to move the coal from the corners and edges of the holds into the central area, making access for the grabs much easier. The trimmer's tool was a long handled shovel. This was clearly filthy and dangerous work. Their shovels, however, also had another more cheery function. These labourers had their own race in the Dartmouth Regatta when the shovels would be used instead of oars!

Ralph Bovey was station master at Kingswear from December 1935 until he retired in May 1954. Born in Teignmouth in 1889, he joined Great Western Railway in 1903 and died in 1974. He lived in Dartmouth and would cross the river on The Mew (the steam passenger ferry) to start work at about 9am. He worked six days a week, finishing at 5.30pm. As trains arrived in Kingswear, they would be unloaded while the engine was turned around. Goods for Dartmouth would be stacked on barrows until they could be taken to the ferry. Goods and parcels for Kingswear were stacked on separate barrows for local delivery.

The photograph shows the station with Mr Hawkes' lorry laden with coal

Jack Eveleigh started working on the railway in Kingswear in June 1937, where he stayed until joining the RAF in 1941. Although he lived close to the station he would arrive by bicycle as he used it during his shift. As a junior porter he was responsible for ensuring that all trains had a tail lamp then checking that these were removed from a carriage before it was taken to the sidings. Immediately before the war the first train to Exeter would be at 8.14am, thereafter trains running every hour. The junior porters had to deliver luggage and parcels to local houses, either on foot with a barrow or by hanging the parcel from the bicycle handlebars. Heavy goods would be taken by van with Jack helping the driver. Between trains he would help generally around the station including cleaning the loos and filling the carriage water tanks from hydrants while they were in the Hoodown sidings.

This view looks north from the footbridge and shows the sidings on the right with the turntable in the middle of the picture.

This photograph looks towards the station with coal cranes on the quayside.

Ronald Knapman was the last signalman to work in the Kingswear signal box and is pictured here watching the railway traffic. The box was built in 1894 with 35 working levers and the signalman even had the luxury of a stool! Alongside was the lamp hut where Jack Eveleigh would service his lamps and polish the brass fittings. There was a 40 gallon drum of paraffin for refuelling the lamps. Eddie Smales remembers that the 1055 Kingswear train would reach Paddington at 1655. Not bad for steam! Very soon after the end of the war, a revised train timetable came into force offering 14 trains to and from Kingswear on weekdays.

KINGSWEAR RAILWAY 1940-1950

Douglas Roper drew up a list of the various tasks required to keep the railway and passenger ferry running. Many of the names are familiar and crop up elsewhere in this book.

STAFF

Station Master	Mr Ralph Bovey
Station Foreman	Mr Harry Langford
Signalmen	Bill Perry, Tom Marshall, Reg Selway (relief)
Shunters	Bill Selly, Bert Smith, Reg Selway, Frank Congdon, and Bill Thomas
Britannia Crossing	Bob Ashton and Mrs Ashton
Porters	Albert Philips, Bill Harvey, George Fisher, Bill Bearman, Fred Roper
Lad Porters	Douglas Roper and Ron Pollard
Ticket Collectors	Wilfred Tottle, Wilf Wotton, Sam Pippin, Mrs Percy
Crane Drivers	Bert Smith, Reg Selway
Shire horse	Sam Hawke
Examiner	Sam Cooper

Reg Selway was a World War I hero earning the Military Cross for bravery. His medals have recently been given to Kingswear Parish Council and are displayed in the Sarah Roope Trust Rooms.

DARTMOUTH FERRY "THE MEW" 1940-1950

STAFF

Mew Skippers	Bob Legge, George Clements, Bill Harris, Bob Chase
Deck Hands	Fred Lye, Dusty Miller, Bill Hoare, Paddy Bardew, Sam Pink, Frank Coombes
Bookstall	Bill Kelland
Pontoon Keeper	Charley Pepperal

This photograph shows Bill Kelland in his newspaper, book and sweet stall at Kingswear station in February 1971. The following day the stall closed after 40 years. Bill Kelland was also Scout Master for the Kingswear Group.

In his 'Growing up in wartime Kingswear', Reg Little remembers that 'at the time the Station Master was one of the most important men in the Parish. We used to give the engine-drivers a hand to turn the engine round on the turntable, and then they would often give us a ride on the footplate across the bridge to Hoodown and back to the station. I have ridden on the King George V and several other famous engines while thus employed. Health and Safety Regulations have certainly spoiled a lot of children's fun!'

As the Crossing Keeper at Britannia Halt, Bob Ashton was responsible for opening and closing the gates, as well as setting the signals. The signal hut was in front of the cottage and adjacent to the railway lines. The signal levers were all polished steel. Maurice Ashton would help his father work these heavy stiff levers, but there was always a duster instantly available to remove any grubby fingerprints from the shiny metal! He remembers that the crossing was busy all

the time with many trains to and from Kingswear and coal being taken to Torquay Gas Works and supplies coming in for the swollen population. At the end of the day, Mr Ashton would cross to Dartmouth to The Floating Bridge Inn for his evening pint. The ferry continued until late in the evening while the trains stopped at 7pm.

Britannia Halt

There was much activity around Britannia Cottage. Old Rock Inn next to the ferry acted as a first aid station, with four doctors in residence, as well as a tool store for the US troops. The troops would frequently pop in for a cup of tea and Edith Ashton seemed to be constantly putting the kettle on. When she was not making tea, she did the ironing for this group of soldiers stationed at Noss!

...Ness on the Dart

Joyce Anderson, nee Ashton, also helped with the ironing. She had a cherished autograph book in which GS Salter of the 8th Devons wrote the following poem:

We are the heroes of the night
We do not shrink from any fight
We are the Glorious eigths
On to the battlefield we marched
Our flags were flying high
It's death before dishonour
And that's our victory cry
Our motto is an old one
From other days
It's Semper Fidelas
In other words ever faithful
It's true in many ways
March on, true Devons, march on
The fight has just begun
Nothing is too much trouble
And by us is always done.

By and large the ferries kept going as best they could during the war. Most of them were steam-powered and had adequate supplies of coal.

The Mew was the Railway Steam Ferry and served as the regular passenger ferry across the Dart from 1907 to 1954. Eventually she retired gracefully with all honours, together with a serenade of sirens and rockets. The large crowd remembered her with affection as serving a very important role in daily life and activities.

In 1940 she attempted to help with the Dunkirk Evacuation when there was a call for small boats to rescue the troops. Reg Little noted that all the craft accepted for the evacuation moored alongside each other on the quay opposite the Post Office which is now Fulford's Estate Agent at Dartmouth. There they were issued with primus stoves, food, water containers, life jackets, and spare petrol. In order to make haste up the English Channel, The Mew was also loaded with as much coal as she could possibly carry. Her top speed was only about 10 knots and after reaching the other end of the Channel was rather sadly deemed to be not up to the job of evacuating soldiers from the French beaches. The crew must have felt very demoralised. As she didn't go over to Dunkirk she was used to unload bigger ships at Dover, so her trip was not entirely without purpose. She arrived back in the Dart about ten days later. This picture shows her carrying apparently excessive numbers of troops towards Dartmouth. Perhaps they had arrived in Kingswear by train and were completing their onward journey.

After the Slapton disaster, in which many US forces were lost during an exercise, a heavily damaged tank landing craft limped into the Dart for repairs. Terry Satchell was on the lower ferry at the time as the stricken vessel crept up river. The ferry was required to hove-to mid river to let it past.

Thanks to Rob Little for this photo of the Lower Ferry dated 28 August 1945 working well as a passenger ferry in the absence of any cars! This reflected the reduction in car traffic with the imposed petrol rationing. Foot passengers were, therefore, encouraged to use the lower ferry and a shelter was apparently erected on the float for their convenience. The lease of the ferry rights was owned by The General Estates Co Ltd from 1932 to 1946 and included two tugs Hauley I and Hauley II. Their names reflect one of the Dart's most famous seamen, John Hauley a 14th century campaigner, who famously attacked French merchant ships in the English Channel.

The above picture shows Hauley I and its pontoon loading at Kingswear in the early years of the war. The walkway referred to below is visible on the left. Passengers and cars would pay for their crossing on the Kingswear side. Ken Langworthy was the ticket collector for many years and had a hut with a fire on the right side of the slipway, adjacent to the Royal Dart Hotel. There was also a gate, again seen on the left, that was closed at night and could control large numbers of leaving passengers to ensure everyone paid! There was no ticket collector on the Dartmouth side.

Dartmouth Council built three passenger launches to supplement the Lower and Passenger Ferries between the wars, and these ran for another 15 years or so after the war. They were called Reliance Perseverance and Newcomen. They would work between the Embankment on the Dartmouth side and Kingswear slipway. There was a walkway on the left side of the slipway that continued just round the corner of the wall. This allowed these launches to load and unload passengers even if the Lower Ferry was also there. Mr Clements was skipper for many years and the fare was 1d! This launch is heading across to the Kingswear side of the river.

Here the Higher Ferry is starting its journey across the river. The slipway on the Kingswear side is adjacent to the Britannia Halt railway crossing. It was in the Keeper's Cottage that secret talks were held in the run up to D-day.

Bob Ashton was the keeper at the time and it was many years later that he reported the story that General Montgomery, General Eisenhower, Lord Mountbatten and General Patten held their high level talks in his home. The discussions were of course top secret and their precise nature is not known and probably never was. However, it seems that the planning of D-day was definitely on the agenda as his son, Maurice, reflects.

Bob Ashton's son-in-law, Vic Anderson, worked on an ammunition supply ship, the Goumier, moored on the river. After one of the bombing raids, when bombs narrowly missed the ship, Vic collected the dead and stunned fish which had floated to the surface of the river! Nothing wrong with a free supper!

References:
C R Potts – The Newton Abbot to Kingswear Railway
Growing up in wartime Kingswear: reminiscences of Reg Little.
The Dartmouth Chronicle
Passenger Steamers of the River Dart – Clammer and Kittridge
Great Western Railway Journal 1998

And thanks to
Gillian Bovey for the station photos
Don Collinson & Maurice Ashton for other photographs

13. The Church

Michael Stevens has written an excellent and comprehensive book on The Church of St Thomas of Canterbury. He has kindly allowed me to reproduce here aspects of his book that relate to the war years.

'The year 1939 dawned full of foreboding, with the spectre of war drawing closer, yet in spite of preparations for conflict ordinary humdrum daily events still continued and Kingswear was no exception. The entrance to the graveyard at Cemetery Corner was much improved and enhanced by the erection of strong stone piers and wrought iron gates and railings, whilst on a more cheerful note the vicar, the Rev F H Keyworth, composed a superb hymn "Carol of the Kingswear Bells: Gabriel, Mary, Michael" which he set to music using A B and C flat, which were the pitches of the bells and it was played at the dedication service.

Three bells in the ancient tower
Weave their mystic rime
Two archangels great of power
Mary sweet of chime.

Gabriel

I the Ave Mary bell
Gabriel crystal clear
Down on knee from heaven he fell
Greeting Mary dear.

When my silver tones resound
Christian people tell
Of that Maiden Gabriel found
Close by Nazareth's well.

Mary

"Lo the hand maid of the Lord"
Mary Maid am I
She who did with sweet accord
Slander's breath defy.

"Full of grace" my clear notes ring
On the obedient ear;
"Jesus only" hear them sing
For my Son most dear.

Michael

"Who is like unto the Lord"
*Michael is my name. ***
Strong my arm 'gainst Satan's horde
Thrusting them to shame.

For the living and dead
Deep my bourdon falls,
Where the souls of men find Bread
In these prayer-filled walls.

Three bells in the ancient tower –
(Hear our mystic rime) –
Two archangels great of power,
Mary sweet of chime.

Come, good people, kiss Christ's feet
Where His grace is found,
Here where saints and angels meet
On God's holy ground.

The name Michael in Hebrew means "Who is like unto God"

In August the port was honoured by the arrival of the Royal Yacht "Victoria and Albert III" with their majesties and the two princesses aboard on a two day visit to the Royal Naval College. However, Kingswear's church bells were still under repair and unable to join their sister churches in Dartmouth with merry peals of welcome but two prominent Kingswear churchmen, Mr A Hine Haycock and Sir Harold Clayton, were invited aboard the Royal Yacht to meet their majesties. The bells were ready by October when they were blessed at a service by the vicar but there was little to celebrate as war had been declared on 3 September 1939. The village along with her larger neighbour, Dartmouth, pressed ahead with the activities of war, with several churchmen taking an active part in civil defence and the services.

The trauma and anxieties of war brought increased congregations and in February, after eighteen months silence, the 1897 clock in the tower was reborn with new chimes that rang bright across the harbour. Strangely a month or so before this event her sister clock in St Saviour's church tower felt she had also earned a refit and 'struck' in sympathy. Her hands stopped at different times, causing much confusion to passing strangers, unaware of her trenchant mood. However the vicar of Dartmouth, the Rev Shell, was able to negotiate with the Kingswear clock's repairers that on completion they would decamp to Dartmouth to complete the clock repairs there, and restore the status quo.

The fortunes of war had not been over-kind to Great Britain with the loss of France and Dunkirk and the country strove to re-arm, first for defence and then for offence. Then in late 1940 two bombs narrowly missed the village, destroying the cottage on the corner of Slappers Hill and Hoodown Farm. This was followed by a much more serious raid in September 1942, when the College was struck and a collier, a mechanical grab on the river sank and the shipyard of Messrs Philip & Son Ltd at Noss heavily damaged. In all 25 people were killed, 20 at Noss shipyard and among the casualties were some members of Kingswear's congregation.

A plaque was erected as a memorial to those who died but when the shipyard closed in 2000 the plaque was repositioned in the church to the right of the First World War memorial.

On a happier note some local girls were married in the church to members of H M forces and two girls married Free French sailors who were based in Kingswear. The Reverend Keyworth was frequently in conversation with the French sailors and told their Padre he could use the church each Ascension Day. All the children from Kingswear Primary School used to process down to the church to take part in the special services.

In 1941 the Secretary of the Parochial Church Council reported at the Annual Church Meeting that "the meetings of the PCC had been reduced to one a year by reasons of the blackout and wartime conditions. Nevertheless the life of the Church has continued unaltered". The lack of meetings sadly means that little is recorded by way of minutes during the war years although much ad hoc business must have been conducted. One feels that the arrival of the King and Queen in Kingswear by special train in May 1942 would have received a mention were it not for the next meeting of the PCC being delayed until April 1943. The Rev Keyworth composed the words and music of a number of hymns, notably one for our patron Saint Thomas Becket to be sung at the patronal festival in July and a War Hymn sung in the church during the war years:

Lord Christ who died to make men free
Whose service is true liberty
Hold through thy servants in thy care
In land and sea, in Gods wide air;
That each may with a carefree mind
In life or death fulfilment find.

Winged spirits held by Michael's helm
Who did the devils hordes o'er whelm,
Upon the rainbow walls of light
And drove them down in headlong flight
Your heavenly aid to all afford

Who served the cause of freedom's Lord

Blest Saints upon the streets of gold
Employed in service manifold
Whose prayer is all that men may find
True liberty in heart and mind
Your prayers and freedom loving power
Upraise in freedoms darkest hour.

Holiest in threefold grace revealed
Within whose knowledge lies revealed
The unfolding of salvations plan
Thy purpose good for rebel man
Then friend and foe at last agree
Their service pure to render thee.

At the February 1948 meeting of the Parochial Church Council the vicar proposed "A War Shrine to commemorate the men of Kingswear who died on service in the 1939 – 1945 War". This was to be a small oak tablet in keeping with the War Shine commemorating the fallen of the 1914 – 1918 War and placed next to it. He had obtained a diagram from Messrs G Maile & Co. of London of what he had in

mind, the estimated cost being £28 although it was subsequently reported to cost "rather more".

Reg Little was in the choir with his brothers. He recalls that there were at least twenty choristers in all. There would be three services each Sunday plus Sunday school. Thriving whist drives helped support an excellent social side which continued throughout war.

Reg also remembers that Vicar Frederick Hector Keyworth was well liked, and wrote many wartime hymns as above as well as tunes. He also 'played the organ beautifully' and welcomed the French soldiers. Vicar Keyworth spoke French but often the French servicemen would go to the Catholic Church in Dartmouth.

Jack Little was also in the choir and would go to choir practice at least once a week. He would then sing at the 11 o'clock Sunday morning service and also at evensong at 3 o'clock in the afternoon; earlier than traditionally for blackout reasons. There was also Holy Communion at 8am. Jack describes Mr Keyworth, a bachelor vicar, as a 'real vicar and a gentleman'. He thinks of him as a clever musician, organ player, hymn writer and composer. Jack was also a server to the good congregations that Mr Keyworth would attract.

One morning after the clocks changed, Jack arrived early to open up the church for the 8am service. He was very surprised that the vicar was not there already as he was usually in good time. Jack set about getting everything ready then went back into the vestry only to discover a note from the vicar on the table. It read 'where is my congregation – shame on Kingswear!' It turned out that the vicar had advanced his clock by two hours not one!

Pat Henshall remembers Rev Keyworth with great fondness. 'He was a lovely man and a real gentleman'. He was nearing retirement at that time and never married. When Pat and Eric went to discuss their wedding in Kingswear Church, the vicar would vacate his large comfy armchair, where he always sat, for the young bride-to-be. He then ordered his housekeeper to give the couple his dried fruit ration for their cake. When their daughter, Jan, was born, the Vicar appeared with a large bunch of flowers from his garden.

Margaret Fabian would go to Sunday school at the Sarah Roope rooms. The attending children would have attendance cards which would get stamped each week. However she soon discovered that the Methodist Sunday School, which was held at the Old School House at the bottom of Wood Lane, got bigger and better stamps, so she went there as well! Her grandmother was verger at St Thomas of Canterbury, so one had to go to morning service every Sunday!

As well as being a barber and shopkeeper, another string to Charlie Heal's bow was role as Verger to St Thomas' Church during the time of the well respected and loved Rev Keyworth. Margaret Heal's mother was responsible for washing the surplices. The sight of all these 'ghostly' white gowns neatly pegged out on the washing line proved to be very comical to a young Margaret!

Margaret Heal recalls that as verger, her father, Charlie Heal was required to light the church stove on Saturday evening, and then be up at 5am on Sunday to stoke it up and help to make a chilly church bearably warm! Sunday school for Margaret would then take place in the Trust rooms, followed by morning service in the church itself at 11am. There was a further session of Sunday school at 2.20pm before evensong at 6.30pm. Was Sunday a day of rest for either the vicar or verger? On Good Friday morning, however, her father would bring Margaret a freshly cooked, still warm, hot cross bun from Mr Stanleick the baker's shop next door.

Margaret Heal married George Rickard from Cornwall on 1 September 1945, making them the first couple to get married in the church after the end of the war.

A former Vicar of Kingswear the Rev Dowland must have been deeply saddened by the news of the death of his son John Noel on active service, yet immensely proud of his achievements during the war. The Paignton Western gazette published the following on 22 January 1942:

John Noel Dowland
6 November 1914-13 January 1942

Squadron leader John Noel Dowland was awarded the George Cross for his gallantry in defusing a bomb which had fallen on a grain ship SS Kildare in Immingham Docks on 11 February 1940. The bomb proved difficult to defuse as it had embedded itself at an extreme angle in the main deck. The citation which appeared in the London Gazette on the 7th January 1941 noted he displayed "conspicuous courage and devotion to duty in circumstances of exceptional danger and difficulty" when defusing a bomb on a trawler in June 1940.

The Commonwealth War Graves Commission records that Wing Commander John Noel Dowland, Service number 33239, died on 13 January 1942 age 27. He was buried in the Capuccini Naval Cemetery in Malta.

References:
St Thomas of Canterbury Kingswear by Michael Stevens and Don Collinson
Michael's book is available in the Church or through FRoST – the Friends of St Thomas.
Commonwealth War Graves Commission website

14. Wartime Rationing

During the War the British government introduced food rationing to make sure that everyone received their fair share of the limited food which was available. The Atlantic convoys bringing supplies to Great Britain were being decimated by the German navy but especially by the U boats. This prevented many ships from delivering their cargoes and caused a colossal loss of men and ships.

On National Registration Day on 29 September 1939, every householder had to fill in a form giving details of the people who lived in their house. Food rationing actually started in 1940 and continued until 1954. Initially, only a few foods were rationed, but more were added to the list as the war continued. The amount of food that was rationed varied through the war and additional allowances were given to certain groups. Everybody was given a ration book, which included coupons for clothes. It was necessary to register at a shop who would then be your supplier of rationed food.

A typical ration for one person each week might be:
3 pints of milk
2oz of tea – (this would have been approximately 15 teabags but these were a much later invention!)
8oz of sugar
4oz of butter or fat
Meat to the value of 1/- or 1/2d which would perhaps buy a pork chop and 3-4 sausages
(1/- or 1 shilling is equivalent to 5p now)
1 egg – 1 packet of dried egg powder was also available every 4 weeks
1oz cheese, but 2oz for manual workers

8oz of sweets each month.

Dried milk was sometimes called household milk. It was mixed with water, and then stirred or whisked vigorously to produce a liquid which was meant to be like fresh milk!

A 'points' scheme was introduced for some foods, for example biscuits and jam, as well as tinned meat, dried pulses and dried fruit. Each person was allowed 20 points a month. Young children, expectant and nursing mothers could receive cod-liver oil, orange juice and milk from welfare clinics. Many people were actually better fed during food rationing than before the war as people who were used to a poor diet now increased their intake of protein and vitamins as they received the same ration as everybody else.

The food shortages meant that people had to adapt to new eating patterns. Consumption of meat, fat, eggs and sugar was much less than before the war. White bread was no longer available when the National Loaf and brown bread became the norm. The Ministry of Food gave advice through radio broadcasts and recipe leaflets to the population about how to make the best of the food that was available.

One such recipe was for a vegetable dish - THE WOOLTON PIE
This was named after Lord Woolton who was the Minister of Food, the recipe has been converted to metric weights to allow the reader to more easily try it at home!

500g Potatoes
500g Cauliflower
500g Swede
500g Carrots
1 tsp Marmite
25g 0atmeal
4 Spring onions
750g Potatoes
25g Cheese

Method
1. Dice and boil 500g of potatoes, cauliflower, swede and carrots in salted water.
2. Strain the vegetables, and save 200ml of cooking water.
3. Arrange the cooked vegetables in a large pie dish.
4. Add the Marmite and oatmeal to the vegetable water and boil until thickened.
5. Pour the thickened liquid over the vegetables.
6. Add the chopped spring onions.
7. Boil and mash the remaining potatoes.
8. Top the pie with mashed potato and a little grated cheese.
9. Heat the pie in a moderately hot oven until golden brown (approximately 1 hour).
10. Serve with brown gravy.

Clothing rationing also came in 1941. Each person was allowed 66 coupons per year. As an example a jacket would be 13 coupons and a shirt 5. The coupons would be exchanged for the article together with the cost of the item. The ability to make and remake clothes was so important and hand-me-downs proved to be essential. Edna Knapman remembers that Mrs Bartlett (with whom she lived at Mount Pleasant after evacuation from London) made all the children's clothes during the war.

Whilst at school, Margaret Fabian would go to her Grandmother's house at 9 Contour Heights for lunch every day. There was always enough to eat and she often remembers having cold meat and potatoes for her midday meal. She also recalls her mother winning a hare in a raffle with a resultant casserole! The jam came in tins rather than jars, Margaret recalls, which were opened with a tin opener that left a jagged sharp edge, then the jam went mouldy very quickly!

New shoes were hard to get, she remembers, and that there were always holes in the soles of their shoes, even though there was a cobbler in the village. Folks often had wooden clogs which were available in Dartmouth as they were not rationed. When asked about wartime clothes Margaret replied with a chuckle – 'liberty bodice and gym slips!' There were also lots of hand-me-downs from her cousins. Silk from parachutes could be made into wonderful underwear and slips! The heavier grey cloth that was used for barrage balloons was converted into a canopy so the family could walk to the outside loo undercover!

Many houses did not have gas or electricity so relied on oil lamps, especially Mrs Weeks just along the road from Margaret. Christmas time saw many second hand toys but her predominant childhood memories are of fun with all her family members around her.

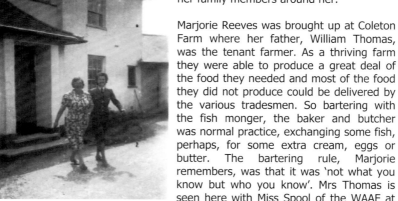

Marjorie Reeves was brought up at Coleton Farm where her father, William Thomas, was the tenant farmer. As a thriving farm they were able to produce a great deal of the food they needed and most of the food they did not produce could be delivered by the various tradesmen. So bartering with the fish monger, the baker and butcher was normal practice, exchanging some fish, perhaps, for some extra cream, eggs or butter. The bartering rule, Marjorie remembers, was that it was 'not what you know but who you know'. Mrs Thomas is seen here with Miss Spool of the WAAF at Coleton Barton farm. Marjorie continues – 'It was about this time that Mother was asked to be responsible for taking in emergency food stocks for all Kingswear. She had to have a special identity card with her photo on, and all the supplies were under our stairs - very basic food, tinned beef, dried biscuits, packets of sugar, tinned margarine and dried milk. This was in case of a German invasion. Thankfully, it never had to be used. I must say we were very glad of the bags of sugar at times, when the Officer came to inspect the stock he would say, 'Another damaged pack, Mrs Thomas?'

Pat Henshall does not remember much of the impact of rationing, although her father would often come home with farm produce if he had been doing a plumbing job on one of the farms. When I asked her about rationing, her response was 'I still do!' and remains reluctant to throw things away. Terry Satchell remembers always feeling hungry during the period of rationing and it was essential to supplement the diet whenever possible. This was usually with rabbits that could be shot or trapped. One local fellow made good use of his ferret. Terry's father also had an allotment on the Hoodown side of the creek which helped to provide a substantial part of the family's vegetables. The children were expected to help gather seaweed from the creek as fertiliser, but also to collect manure from Mr Job's farm just round the corner. Scrumping apples was always a boy's challenge but expect a firm clip across the head if you were caught. Sneaking into a field to grab a swede or turnip and slicing pieces off with a penknife was reality then, but does not particularly appeal to him now. When the Americans arrived things started to look up for the youngsters of Kingswear. The US food supplies were substantially better and more varied than those of the locals. Terry recalls a US jeep and trailer coming into the village from their base at Lupton and the GIs distributing sweets, chocolate and chewing gum for the kids and offering cartons of 200 cigarettes for their parents.

Ros Little recalls that rationing changed from time to time. She worked in the Dartmouth and Kingswear branches of the Co-operative where a special girl would deal with the customer's ration books. She remembers that many people kept chickens so that eggs were fairly easy to get. Rabbits were also readily available to supplement the meagre ration of fresh meat. She said that 'we never went without anything we really needed' and that 'we never seemed short'. There was 'always enough even though a little meat had to go a long way'. Butter, cheese and lard were the hardest food stuffs to obtain.

"We want not only the big man with the plough but the little man with the spade to get busy this autumn. Let 'Dig for Victory' be the motto of everyone with a garden,"
Rob Hudson, Minister for Agriculture, in October 1939.

Many people would grow their own vegetables. The Hoodown side of Waterhead Creek between the houses was largely divided into allotments. Mr Hawke grew vegetables that side of the water which he would then sell in the shop which was run by Mrs Hawke and their son. Mr Hawke also had a horse that helped shunt railway coal trucks around Kingswear station.

Nova Varney recalls that her father, Charlie Bovey, who worked as the gardener and chauffeur at Oversteps (now High Springs), grew many vegetables and fruit on Mr Flamank's land. In fact, she says, 'enough for the whole village including white raspberries'.

Nova Varney was allowed 2oz sweets per week as part of her ration. She would go to Mr Hawke's shop (now Ashleigh House) where she would spend some time choosing what to buy. In the end she would select the sweets that would last the longest!

'You always ate what you were given'   Nova recalls, but adds that there was always enough to eat. Her father, Charlie Bovey, also had a boat and was able to go out around the Mewstone to catch fish, when he was able to get enough 'torpedo juice' for the engine! There were always rabbits and pheasants he would shoot to add to the family's menu.

Mrs Heal had a full schedule too. As well as her own three children she took in two evacuated girls from Eltham in London. Later there were two RAF men (one was called Bob, and he came from Bournemouth. Margaret Heal took a holiday with Bob and his wife after the war) and two WAAF girls, one called Daphne. Fortunately the house had five large bedrooms. Mrs Heal was required to provide dinner, bed and breakfast for the billeted troops for which she received a weekly fee. She would also have needed their ration books in order to buy enough food. The family and lodgers would all eat together around the dining table which doubled up as an air raid shelter of the Morrison type. She remembers her mother as 'a good cook' who 'always produced a good meal' although they all missed fruit which was very difficult to obtain. Dried and tinned fruit was a real luxury. Meat was also heavily rationed but local farmers came door to door offering rabbits for 'about a shilling.' Mrs Heal would skin and gut them and was able to sell the skins 'for a pittance' to a man who came to the door.

References:
Arthur Clamp 'Dartmouth & Kingswear during WW2
Women's Voluntary Service website
British Nutrition Foundation

15. The Dartmouth Chronicle

The Dartmouth and South Hams Chronicle had been published every week for 85 years by the start of the war in 1939 and continues today offering local news to the population around the Dartmouth area.

1939
The Dartmouth Chronicle's first edition following the outbreak of war filled two columns with the news of the evacuated children from Acton in London, who found themselves allocated to homes in Kingswear, Dartmouth and the other villages to the west. The mobilisation of the Fire Brigade was reported and the order that the police would ensure that lights were obscured as part of the essential blackout.

The start of petrol rationing was about to have an impact on civilian life as well. If you owned a car you were entitled to a petrol ration book. The amount of fuel you could obtain was dependant on the horsepower of your vehicle. You could apply via the Post Office for an extra allowance, however, if you thought the basic entitlement was inadequate.

In mid September the Kingswear Scoutmaster, Aubrey Hamilton, was married to Marjorie Grant. As the bride and groom left St Saviour's church in Dartmouth after the ceremony, a Guard of Honour was formed by Kingswear Cubs, Scouts and Sea Scouts. A bridesmaid, the matron of honour and sister of the groom were unable to attend owing to Air Raid Precaution duties.

On October 11 1939 'Looker on' of Kingswear wrote to The Dartmouth Chronicle to complain about a man-hole cover in Wood Lane. It had been broken some months before and despite numerous complaints to Totnes Rural District Council no action had been taken. The correspondent continued:

'What do we pay rates for? Is it 1839 or 1939? If someone should break a limb or get an attack of diphtheria who will be responsible? What do we employ Medical Officers of Health for?
Yours etc
Looker On

Mr Hawke, the coal merchant, was reported as explaining that the charge for coal in Dartmouth would rise from 2s 8d per cwt to 3s per cwt. After delivery to Kingswear by collier, the coal had to be transported across the river. Pre-war Dutch colliers had been used but these were now not available. Alternative ships or rail transport had increased delays so the transport costs had risen from 9s per ton to 22s.

On 24 November it was reported that £30 had been raised towards the restoration of the three bells at Kingswear Parish Church. A bazaar was held in the Trust Room and the proceeds boosted the fund to £330. This was now just £50 short of the required amount to pay off the outstanding balance. The bells, Gabriel, Mary and Michael had been refurbished by John Taylor in Loughborough.

Meanwhile, the Kingswear Red Cross working Party was reported as sending 90 items 'including clothes for hospitals and comforts for the Forces'. The Working Party met in the Trust Rooms with the permission of the Vicar Rev F H Keyworth.

Early in December 1939 the Parish Council's discussions reached the newsprint. Mr H Piper of Dartmouth Urban Electric Supply Co offered to reduce the charges for Kingswear's street lighting by 10s 7d for September and by £5 11s for the last quarter of the year.

Just before Christmas the newspaper observed that, although the shops feared that the blackout would disturb trade, an increase in sales had been realised. Mr Pook, a gentleman's outfitter in Dartmouth, felt that travel restrictions meant that shoppers were reluctant to go to Torquay and possibly return during the blackout, when local retailers offered more convenience.

1940
Early in February 1940 three Brixham fishermen had a lucky escape by the Castle Ledge Buoy off the Kingswear side of the Dart estuary. The fishing smack, Valerian, was perilously close to the rocks in heavy seas and not responding to her helm when the rebounding waves pushed the boat out of

harm's way. This meant that Skipper Beaumont was forced to guide his vessel between the rocky shore and the Mewstone. Huge waves broke over the boat during this passage. Back in Brixham, Skipper Beaumont said 'when death stares you in the face it makes you do what you can to escape it. This was the worst experience I've had in my trawling career'. The Valerian was one of only two Brixham smacks still working and had won the King George Challenge Cup and the Alfred Wallace Vancouver Memorial Cup more times than any other smack since the Great War.

The following week The Chronicle reported that 'after being silent for 18 months the clock on the tower of Kingswear Parish Church chimed the hours and quarter hours once again this week'. The face had also been repainted and the hands re-gilded.

Meanwhile, during an ARP rehearsal high explosive, gas and incendiary bombs were 'dropped' on Kingswear. Imaginary fires caused much damage in Fore Street. The Dartmouth Fire Brigade came via the Lower Ferry to help, the 'casualties' were taken to the Village Hall for their 'wounds' to be tended. Gas bombs were 'dropped' on Higher Contour Road but were rapidly decontaminated. A broken electricity cable was repaired by the Dartmouth Electricity Repair Squad, while Mr W Fairweather and Mr F Hodsdon were in the Report Centre (Village Hall) and Dr Hope-Gill and Mrs Melville supervised the First Aid Post. The newspaper noted that 20 personnel were involved in the exercise.

Captain Bennett Lawson, 67, was a retired sea captain who lived on the yacht Norda as a winter caretaker for the Dartmouth owner Mr G Lambert. Having not been seen for several days, Mr Lambert visited the boat to discover Mr Lawson's body. The boat was moored in Kingswear creek at the time. A post mortem confirmed death due to natural causes and the Coroner, Mr Ernest Hutchings, declared an inquest unnecessary.

A letter signed 'a mother' provoked response from Mr Phillpott of Kingswear as well as Editorial column inches! The 'mother' declared that *girls and young women are always to be seen about our streets dressed beyond their station in life'* and *'behaving in every brazen way possible in order to attract the attention of our men in uniform causing most disgraceful behaviour'*. Mr Phillpott thought the worst aspect of the matter was the fact that the letter was anonymous. The Editor noted that *'the girls of today are no better and no worse than those in 1920 or 1900'* and that *'those who live longest may see more changes when peace is restored. No great war ever leaves a nation in thought and outlook where it found it'*. Wise words indeed. Did 'the mother' feel thoroughly rebuked?

Mr J Melville was the billeting officer for Kingswear. He informed The Dartmouth Chronicle on 17 June 1940 that 107 evacuee children from Elton in London were expected to arrive in the village on the following Sunday and that accommodation had been found for all of them. It was anticipated that the younger children would be absorbed into Kingswear School while the older ones would be educated in Dartmouth. It turned out that their first exciting outing in sunny Devon would be to Goodrington with the Kingswear Methodist Church.

Mr Nicholl of The Chalet, Kingswear wrote to the paper in July. The Air Ministry had asked him *'to take what steps are necessary to destroy peregrine falcons between Berry Head and Plymouth'.* These now treasured and admired birds have a liking for pigeons. Homing pigeons were often used to convey important messages from boats with radio silence, from the army and from Coastal Command aircraft. Mr Nicholl concludes his letter by saying that *'as a member of the Devon Bird Watching and Preservation Society I wish to make it quite clear that nothing except the safety of the country would make me take such steps'.* He also stressed the success the Society had achieved in preserving this fine falcon over the previous years.

Issues regarding the Lower Ferry appeared once again in January 1941. Kingswear Parish Council presented a number of points for discussion:

1. Fares should be collected while the ferry is in transit to avoid congestion on reaching Kingswear.
2. The float should not run continuously as this has caused delays
3. The float should run until 7pm then the launch should take over until 10pm. This suggestion was because of the danger of crossing the river in the blackout and the reduced number of cars using the ferry in the evening
4. Concern about the floats and tugs not being kept in running order.

The point raised in item 1 related to the practice of a ticket collector boarding the ferry as it arrived at the slipway to collect fares, which clearly created some delays. This practice is seen in the 1930s film 'Sons of the Seas' which was filmed largely in Kingswear and Dartmouth.

On a happier note the Kingswear evacuee children were given a treat organised by Rev Keyworth. He arranged a cinema show in Kingswear Hall with the help of Mr and Mrs Melville, Miss E Haywood the school mistress, Mr Fairweather and Mrs Tabb. The show included Charlie Chaplin in 'Charlie's Elopement' and 'Popeye'. Tea followed which was 'greatly appreciated'.

1941

The Dartmouth Chronicle of 29 January 1941 had a headline:

KINGSWEAR'S FIREFIGHTING CALL
FIRST VOLUNTEERS ENROLLED ON THE SPOT
PLACE FOR WOMEN IN THE RANKS

In the Village Hall, with Mr Fairweather as chairman, about fifty members of the village attended a firefighting meeting. Incendiary bombs were described by Mr Kauntze, Head Warden of the Totnes area. He said there were simple ways of dealing with the menace which might seem to be a frightening obstacle   It was suggested that if the incendiary bomb could be buried in earth or mud before it started to burn, that would be the best solution. If it had started to smoulder it could be removed with a long handled shovel and placed in a more convenient situation. Ideally, if it was in a house, it would be thrown out of the window so that it could burn itself out elsewhere rather than setting fire to a house which could become a guiding beacon for enemy aircraft.

It was also hoped to buy as many stirrup pumps for the village as was possible so that any fires that had started could be brought under control. Along with each stirrup pump it was hoped to supply an axe so firefighters could hack away any timber which otherwise might add to the brilliance and duration of the blaze. Mr Fairweather also requested that anyone who owned a ladder would be prepared to let the ARP know so that it could be used in case of emergency. This was in accordance with the appeal of Mr Herbert Morrison, the Home Secretary.

Parties would be formed to fight the fires. Their duties would not be very arduous but hopefully quite simple. When an alert signal was blown, a member of each party would patrol and keep a lookout in his own area. If planes were seen overhead he would gain control and when the all clear sounded he would finally retire.

In the same edition of The Dartmouth Chronicle of 24 January 1941 another headline declared that the Dart Spitfire was now within reach. Only £750 was needed to complete the fund of £5000 (at least £230,000 in 2011 terms) thus enabling a Spitfire to be named after Dartmouth and Kingswear. Whilst that good news was being reported, blood donors were still in short supply. People from both Dartmouth and Kingswear should be more willing to step forward to donate blood, the paper explained. The reporter also noted that it was thought by some people that to give blood was a painful and gory business. However Dr Barnett said this was not so although some people still had this impression.

Lighting up and blackout times over Dartmouth and Kingswear were routinely published. In March 1942 the blackout was from 7:34 pm till 7:15 am.

On 23rd May 1941 the headline reads:

MOST HISTORIC WEEK IN 750 YEARS
THE MAYOR TO TAKE THE SALUTE AT TOMORROWS MARCH PAST
KINGSWEAR'S SHARE IN EFFORT TO PAY FOR A WARSHIP

The Dartmouth Chronicle printed a letter from Sir Kingsley Wood, Chancellor of the Exchequer which read –
'I send you my warmest good wishes for the success of Dartmouth and Kingswear war weapons week. A fine result to the first year of the war savings campaign is the best encouragement you can possibly have to redouble our efforts to meet the mounting cost of the war. It is becoming increasingly clear that all of us are in duty bound to spend as little and lend as much to the nation as we possibly can. Selfish spending today can only weaken our war effort. Civic effort is an outstanding value in this vital campaign and I'm sure that the systems of Dartmouth and Kingswear will do their utmost during war weapons week to reach a total of which they may be justly proud.'
signed Kingsley Wood

War weapons week started on Saturday, 24 May and continued through to Saturday 31st which happened also to be Empire Day. The campaign opened on Saturday afternoon with a parade of sailors, soldiers and airmen, ARP units, Home Guard, Red Cross nurses, Boy Scouts and Girl Guides. Members of the

Women's section of the British Legion arranged to sell special badges in both Dartmouth and Kingswear throughout the day. Shop windows and the shop interiors displayed brilliant posters whilst outside a flag day was held with bunting and also a large painting was on offer of a motor launch boat by Mr C Young.

In July 1941 the Ministry of Food's egg control scheme was in a muddle. The scheme intended to offer home produced eggs to housewives on a regular and reasonable basis. However there was a lot of criticism that by the time the eggs were available they were more than a week old. Although the scheme had been going for more than a month it was showing no signs of running smoothly. Producers were not receiving a full price, retailers were not always receiving the eggs that they were expecting and the housewife, apart from paying a high charge, found the eggs she bought were not always as fresh as they should have been.

In an interview with the newspaper, Mr John Coaker of Kingston Farm near Kingswear, who had more than 200 laying hens, expressed his views which were in common with the majority of poultry farmers throughout the country. *'The view that the scheme is impractical, expensive and lacking in results are the first and most obvious points'* Mr Coaker said. *'It is a waste of time and petrol that eggs are conveyed to the packing station to be crated and in some cases the distance from producer to the station was a very large one. Apart from this the eggs are kept on the farm for periods sometimes more than a fortnight before they are collected. Every time the government brings out a scheme'*, Mr Coaker declared, *'the small producer is always the most badly affected. In this case the details are becoming so complicated that the small retailer may be forced to go out of business.'*

During the summer of 1941, the quayside at Kingswear was being extended. This required large amounts of gravel and stone to be delivered. The laden lorries, up to eight a day, would come along the lane at Hoodown, turn around and reverse across the railway line to offload their delivery. Poor 37 year old Ernest Blake of Paignton misjudged this manoeuvre and straddled the railway line just as a train was coming. A collision was inevitable and Mr Blake was hurled from his lorry and drowned in Waterhead Creek.

A coroner's inquest was held in Kingswear Village Hall two weeks later and the whole story was published on 26 September. Mr Letcher of Eastley & Co Solicitors represented Mrs Blake and Mr Easterbrook, solicitor of Paignton, represented the haulage contractors, Diggins, also of Paignton. The coroner was Mr E Hutchings. Numerous witnesses were questioned and cross examined. It appeared that the lorry was pushed 138ft down the line and completely destroyed. Mr Hutchings felt that the railway company and the driver, G Mitchell of Exeter, carried no blame for the accident. The coroner felt that Mr Blake's death was due to extreme negligence. It was possible for drivers to come and go across the lines without any warning systems, yet there were about 25 workmen on the site at the time who could have kept watch. *'What was everyone's job was nobody's job'* the coroner concluded.

Unemployment issues are not just the territory of our times. In October the newspaper stated that thity coal lumpers were out of work in Dartmouth and Kingswear and drawing unemployment benefits. Meanwhile there was increased pressure on farmers to produce more food. Some of these farmers had applied in vain to the Labour Exchange. *'Why labour cannot automatically be made available for other work when one job comes to an end is difficult to understand'* the paper said. *'One more illustration of our failure to use 100% of our available manpower'* it concluded.

Kingswear Red Cross had been busy over the previous three months collecting a total of £80 0s 8d. The Philips Boatyard had collected £21 17s 7d, door to door collections of 1d a week raised £15 2s 8d, a competition by Mrs Melville, 1s 11d and the sale of a budgerigar realised 2s 6d! The working parties had been busy making 443 garments and comforts for Service personnel, together with 700 milk jug covers for the Middle East. A total of 4700 items had been made in the last twelve months. Fortunately a large bale of winceyette fabric was now in store for winter work.

Letcher and Scorer, auctioneers of Dartmouth, held an auction at 'Eastney', Church Hill, in November 1941. Large amounts of mahogany furniture were on offer, together with canteens of silver cutlery, Waterford glass, a Sanderson plate camera, 'Murphy' and 'Pye' mains wireless sets and a 32hp Marmon 8 cylinder coupe motor car of 1930 with 32,000 miles on the clock! The next edition noted that six glass wine goblets fetched 7s each and surmised that *'there are still some optimists who believe that the rich wines of the world will flow freely and cheaply again.'* The 'Murphy' wireless set fetched £13!

1942
This year's Dartmouth and Kingswear Warship Week raised a staggering £122,395 10s 6d. (This equates to over £4 million today!) The hull of a destroyer, HMS Haldon, was the target of the fundraising at £120,000. The Mayor of Dartmouth and Mr W Fairweather, Chairman of Kingswear Parish Council, announced the success to a large jubilant crowd outside the Guildhall. Kingswear had been buzzing with activities all week with an ARP dance, a gala night in the Hall, whist drives, bring-and-buy sales, cake stalls and a contribution of £737 from the Women's Institute alone.

Mr Nicholl of The Chalet found it necessary to write to the newspaper once again in April. The last year's efforts in controlling peregrine falcons had some success, he wrote, but not enough. He reinforced the danger these beautiful birds posed to message bearing pigeons and asked for more help from locals to identify their breeding localities.

An advertisement on page 3 asks   **What do I do...** to get 45lbs extra meat in a year? The answer is rabbits! *'Rabbits can be kept in the smallest yard or garden and the young from one doe can provide 45lbs annually of nourishing and tasty food over and above your normal meat ration.'* If you wanted to know how to buy, house and feed rabbits, you could just write to the Ministry of Agriculture at London WC2 for their leaflet.

THE TWO WORLD WARS REMEMBERED

That was the headline in November 1942. Special Remembrance Day services were held in St Thomas of Canterbury Kingswear and a very large congregation attended the service conducted by the Rev F H Keyworth. Members of the Home Guard, ARP, Red Cross, Boy Scouts, fire guards and Police were present all in uniform. They joined in heartily in the singing of hymns. A memorial service was held at the war shrine for all those who had lost their lives by enemy action in the two world wars with special mention of the Kingswear men. The church had been artistically decorated with autumn leaves, berries and flowers by women in the congregation.

In December there was a report headed:

WOMEN'S PART IN POST WAR PLANNING

describing the Women's Institute annual meeting. Mrs Fenner was re-elected as the President after a proposal by Mrs Hope-Gill and second by Mrs Yates. The Women's Institute had battled hard throughout the year to improve the salvage situation in the village. A great deal of work had been done with the relevant officers at Totnes Rural District Council to help to achieve this. The WI had also worked hard to collect foxglove leaves which were then sent off for preparation into digitalis medicines for heart conditions. In her speech the secretary concluded that *'during 1942 we have endeavoured to carry on and to show that the power and usefulness of Women's Institutes depend on the thought of the members and the united effort which they can make through their organisation. Many and varied opportunities lie ahead, we must seize them eagerly in the belief that as a great democratic federation of countrywomen, we are contributing, not only to the achievement of peace, but also to the planning of the post-war world.'*

1943

In a Public Notice, The Ministry of Fuel and Power outlined coal supplies to households for January, February and March.
1. coal supplies shall not exceed 15cwt during those three months and no supplies may be acquired if stocks already exceed 10cwt
2. coke supplies may not exceed 10cwt per month

Consumers were also reminded that these quantities were maximum and not rations to which they were entitled. Deliveries would depend on local supply and priority given to consumers without stocking facilities.

A whole series of adverts appeared in The Chronicle over the coming months concerning 'The Battle for Fuel'. You would be encouraged to:
- take unburnt coal off the fire at night
- sieve the cinders in the morning and save 2 million tons of fuel a year
- use the poker as little as possible
- guard against draughts to be warmer with a smaller fire
- share your fireside with friends and neighbours

The Dartmouth and Kingswear Hospital was very dependant on gifts, donations and subscriptions to keep their services running in the pre-NHS days. In January they enjoyed a generous donation of vegetables and many individuals and groups, such as local schools, gave silver paper and used stamps. There were generous cash donations from many sources including Prudential Assurance Co of £5 5s and £4 from the Naval College.

HMS Haldon, the destroyer which was adopted by Kingswear and Dartmouth after the Warship Week last year, was to be transferred to the Free French, given a French name and put into service with General de Gaulle's forces, the newspaper explained. This was revealed in a letter from the Admiralty read out to Dartmouth Town Council. If the town did not wish to continue with this adoption, it was possible that their interest could be focused on HMS Dartmouth which was soon to come into service.

Wings for Victory week was now being planned for June. It was hoped to raise £80,000 between Kingswear and Dartmouth to fund sixteen fighter planes. At a meeting in the Guildhall with Mr Fairweather and Howe representing Kingswear, The Mayor of Dartmouth, Mr Row, praised the communities for their *'top of the list'* efforts in the Warship Week and Weapons for War week and was sure they *'would not go to sleep'* in this special project. Kingswear and Dartmouth had been top of the Devon list of percentage savings during the previous fundraising drives. He went on to say that the *'wonderful service, the RAF, that had saved the country during the Battle of Britain and now their planes flew night after night to bomb the Continent to save Britain from being reduced to the state of countries like Poland and Czechoslovakia.'* The Air Ministry *'would present an attractive trophy and log book of the aircraft adopted.'*

The Wings for Victory programme was published in The Chronicle on 9 June. Parades, concerts and dances were planned in Dartmouth, including a fly past of a fighter plane, whilst in Kingswear the week started with a parade of Civil Defences and a Service in the Church. More than 200 members of the Fighting Forces, Civil Defences and youth groups attended the parade and church service. Rev Keyworth spoke of *'the moral and spiritual effect the coming Allied victory would have on the world.'*

During the following days whist drives and a dance were held in the Village Hall. Miss Heywood of Kingswear School arranged a children's fancy dress procession followed by a variety concert. There was a dance on the Friday night to round off the week whilst a selling centre in Fore Street had been open every day. The Kingswear WI had a target of £32 for the week but eventually raised £3103 5s 6d and at a subsequent presentation of certificates, the Mayor of Dartmouth led a *'round of clapping as a tribute to the magnificent and, as far as Dartmouth is concerned, unequalled effort of the group.'*

The headline on 1 October 1943 read:
IMPRESSIVE KINGSWEAR CEREMONY
Mr and Mrs Frank Little presented colours to Kingswear Wolf Cub unit as a memorial to their second son Patrol Leader Herbert George Little who was killed in an air raid a year ago. The colours were blessed and dedicated at Evensong in Kingswear Parish Church when a large congregation assembled for the ceremony and Rev F Keyworth officiated. Members of various youth services, including Boy Scouts from Dartmouth, took part in a parade before the service and they formed a solid phalanx in the centre of the open nave. During the service Mr William Kelland, the assistant scoutmaster, and Mr Little took the

colours and handed them to the Vicar who laid them on the alter to bless them. Prayers followed for the Scout movement, for England and the Empire, and for the repose of the soul of the Scout 'gone home' Herbert George Little.

The Ministry of Food advertised again in the Chronicle at the end of October declaring the national potato reserves for May, June and July 1944. The advert reassured the reader that the Ministry had secured adequate reserves on farms in Great Britain of potatoes for consumption during that period. Growers would offer their best keeping potatoes for this purpose. It was anticipated that they would be offered 15 shillings per ton and the Ministry of Food expected growers to offer promptly at least a quarter of their total production.

At the end of November 1943 a story revealed that a

BORED SOLDIER RAIDS FARMHOUSE

Gunner Joseph Bailey was sentenced to 9 months imprisonment at Devon Quarter Sessions after pleading guilty to charges of breaking and entering Higher Brownstone Farm in Kingswear. He entered the farm on October 12 and stole £6 15s 6d in cash which belonged to Mr Roland Smith, as well as clothing, shoes, stockings and a flapjack valued at £19 14s 10d, the property of the housekeeper of the farm, Miss Frieda Duker.

Bailey who used to work at the farm knew that the building was unoccupied during September and October, even though an employee went there every day to see that things were in order. He had asked a considerable number of soldiers in his unit to go with him and break into the farm but with one exception they refused to have anything to do with the enterprise. PC Wakeham stated in evidence that Bailey, whose wife and five children lived in Hull, had been bound over twice before. He was described as an efficient technical soldier but his character was unsatisfactory and a bad influence on his younger comrades.

1944
June 9 and the headline reads
'Dartmouth on D-Day'
The report continued '*The BBC morning bulletins on Tuesday, June 6, 1944 broke the news to the people of Britain that D-Day had arrived and that the attack against Europe had been launched. People awaited later bulletins eagerly but with complete confidence and obvious enthusiasm. The news was on everyone's lips. Housewives doing their morning shopping stopped to discuss it, men commented on it at work and agreed on the immediate result of the attack over lunch. There was little thought of anything else. News broadcasts throughout the day found wide audiences hanging on every word. As the day went on anyone who picked up fresh news from one or another of the Allied stations related it to every passing acquaintance. In the street, optimism increased. With the fall of evening and nothing but good news coming from the beachhead Dartmouth and Kingswear were hungry for more details'.*

As nine o'clock approached the streets began to empty as King George was due to speak on the radio to his nation. Kingswear Parish Church of St Thomas a

Becket was crowded as Rev Keyworth led a special service of intercession for the invasion troops.

In September the Chronicle reported
'How the Devons led the assault on Europe'.
Capt Donald Leslie spoke to the townspeople of Dartmouth and Kingswear about the Devon Regiment and its triumphant advances on the shell-swept beaches of Normandy. The Devons were applauding the traditions of the past and proud to be part of the British Army which was known to be the best in the world, he said. Capt Leslie went on to describe how the Devons spearheaded the attack on the Normandy beaches. He also described the amassing of the men, embarkation, the gathering of the great invasion armada and finally the last moments before the attack on June 6, the greatest invasion the world had seen. Capt Leslie revealed that the Devons had sustained 300 casualties in June and at one time they were the most advanced troops in a single action. In one encounter, they inflicted 60 casualties on the enemy capturing 120 prisoners and sustaining only one casualty themselves.

The editorial on October 13 discussed a topic that is not completely unknown today! The Mayor had outlined a plan for a greater Dartmouth with carrots of prosperity that would appeal on the Kingswear side of the river. The recent excellent 'fusion' between the two communities, in terms of fund raising for the war effort, was noted. Would a bridge across the river not bond these communities even more and produce a more prosperous place for the returning forces at the end of the war?

With grateful thanks to The Dartmouth Chronicle.

16. Froward Point and Coleton Radar site

As part of the defences of the Brixham and Kingswear peninsula, a version of the newly developed radar system was built to the east of Kingswear. This was designed to detect approaching enemy forces, while any unwanted visitors to Start Bay had the potential of a high explosive welcome from the Brownstone Battery, overlooking the mouth of the River Dart.

RADAR
The name is an acronym derived from RAdio Detection And Ranging. Before radar was devised, RDF or a radio direction finder was able to detect direction but not range. The principle of radar is the transmission of radio waves and the detection of any waves reflected back from objects in their path. The timing of this reflection allows calculation of distance. It was thus able to detect position and movement of ships and aircraft.

Early in the war priority was given to building long range radar stations called Chain Home or CH. These were dotted around the east and west coasts of England. It then became clear that low flying planes capable of mine-laying were not detectable by CH so a modification allowed the radar to 'see' low flying aircraft. This change was called Chain Home Low or CHL.

RAF Kingswear was a CHL site and situated near Coleton Fishacre about 1.5 miles east of the village of Kingswear. This position was chosen in October 1940 by the Air Ministry when the RAF West Prawle site was found to be unsatisfactory in detecting low flying aircraft. RAF Kingswear was operational by 26 June 1941 with the latest power turned aerial. Various technical modifications were incorporated throughout the war. A report in November 1941 suggested that RAF Kingswear achieved a range of 163 miles, although 90 miles was more widely reported. It could detect aircraft up to 15000 feet and had a 360° view so covered the whole of Start Bay and Lyme Bay.

During the war, radar was highly secret and although locals might have been aware of an RAF site, its purpose may have remained mysterious. Thus these radar sites, as well as airfields, were protected by the newly formed RAF Regiment. They arrived in Kingswear in 1943 and it is noted that in 1944 one Officer and 30 ranks were responsible for guarding the site, rising to three times that number before the end of the war. Various Nissen huts were adjacent to the radar installation itself and it is known that the Commanding Officer was billeted at Coleton Farm for a period. Some of the other ranks had accommodation in the adjacent farms. The Nissen huts were used as stores, administration, recreation and generator buildings. There was also an air raid shelter.

URBAN ELECTRIC SUPPLY C? L?.

COUNTERPART.
TO BE RETAINED BY OWNER
FOR REFERENCE.

Consent No........2.
(Owner)

Consent to Erection of Electric Lines.

I/We, MRS. TIVY, of "VILLA", YEALMPTON, SOUTH DEVON.
Estate Agent:- D. M. Waterson,
of CHURSTON FERRERS, SOUTH DEVON.
(hereinafter referred to as "the Owner" which expression includes his heirs
executors administrators successors or assigns where the context so admits) being
the owner of lands situate in the Parish of Brixham U.D.C.
in the County of Devon (hereinafter referred
to as "the said land") shown on the plan annexed hereto (hereinafter referred to
as "the said plan") and thereon coloured pink HEREBY CONSENT to the electric
lines specified in Part I of the Schedule hereto being placed above or below the
said land by the URBAN ELECTRIC SUPPLY CO. LTD. whose principal registered
office is situate at 24-30 Gillingham St. in the County of London
(hereinafter referred to as "the Company") upon the following terms conditions
and stipulations:—

As part of the coastal defence arrangements, Froward Point Battery and, later, Coleton Camp Radar Station were built. Both installations were inevitably quite remote but still required a supply of electricity. The Urban Electric Supply Co. Ltd negotiated with Mrs Tivy, the owner of Kingston Farm, although Mr John Coaker was tenant, for the erection of supply poles across her fields.

Marjorie Reeves remembers that 'By now the camp was fully manned and we had the CO billeted with us. Then a little later a WAF Officer, Miss Spool, came to live with us at home. The WAFs and the RAF boys that were on the camp were billeted around various farms and in Brixham. A transport lorry took them backwards and forwards for the different shifts. They called each day for milk

from the farm. There was no canteen; they just made cups of tea or coffee.'

The Commanding Officer of the Radar station at Coleton Farm gate.

Even before the Commanding Officer of RAF Kingswear was billeted at Coleton Farm, two Corporals were made welcome in the farmhouse.

Corporal Banks and Corporal Reeves were amongst the first guards to patrol this high security site. Their photographs are shown below. They must have made an impact as Corporal Reeves subsequently married Marjorie, daughter of Mr and Mrs Thomas who ran Coleton Farm.

Cpl Banks   Cpl Reeves

Corporal Bernard Reeves was for a while billeted at 3 Kingston Farm Cottages but complained that the lady there was such a poor cook he could not tolerate the food. After that he moved to Boohay Farm which proved to be much more pleasant!

Reg Little recalls that the 'Royal Air Force Radar Station, AME (Air Ministry Experimental) station was at Coleton Fishacre' on the site which is now a car park. It was on the left of the main gate to Coleton Fishacre House. This was one of a chain of early warning stations around the coast of England. They saved us in the Battle of Britain. Very few people nowadays seem to know anything about it. There were several big buildings there and a huge rotating aerial. The Germans tried to bomb it on several occasions. I can remember looking for bombs through the fields when one exploded quite near the station. The first radar station there was in a caravan in 1939 shortly after the war broke out. One of the operators was Ken Burford who was a Hoover agent for Torbay after the war. The Coleton Radar site was closed by the time I left the Army, but there was a radar presence near the top of Hillhead, opposite the present day caravan park, until the mid 1950's. At various times the radar station was guarded by RAF Regiment armoured cars. Numerous air raids tried to target the Radar site. They were very lucky, because bombs aimed at the Radar Station dropped in the next field.'

Reg Little also wrote in the December 2008 Kingswear Historians Newsletter that 'In April 1940 strange shapes began appearing near Coleton Camp'. Reg continues 'When I was thirteen I went round delivering meat for Mr Scoble the butcher on Saturdays on a bike with a basket (like Granville in Open All Hours). On my way to Brownstone Farm I saw massive camouflaged caravans sprouting aerials and a number of RAF personnel in a small plot near the entrance to the farm drive. After a few months, a sentry was put on the lane to the left of the entrance of Coleton Fishacre and a camp was built there. There were a number of Nissen huts and in the middle a Nissen hut with a big rotating dish aerial on a tower above it and a blast wall surrounding it. The electric supply came from the substation at Wood Lane via an overhead cable which later also supplied the Brownstone gun site.

One day in 1941 not long after I started work at 14, a barrage balloon broke loose from its position on the creek sidings and got tangled in Reservoir Field cutting off the supply to the Radar Station. We and the RAF balloon crew from Dartmouth managed to deflate it and get the important supply on again. One afternoon an unexploded bomb dropped on the Radar Station. In the evening we Civil Defence members had to search the surrounding fields as we were told the plane would have had three bombs. None was found. For a while after this the camp was guarded by the RAF Regiment with Daimler armoured cars.

I remember the regiment had a very good dance band. They played at dances in the Kingswear Hall and probably in Brixham. The camp was finally closed in the 1950s and the only connection I had with it later was in organising the Coronation Beacon in 1953. There were not many traces left then.

After one of the raids Terry Satchell was up near the radar site and remembers large amounts of silver paper strips in the hedges, presumably dropped by the German planes to try to deceive the radar system.

After the Radar unit was dismantled in the 1950s the area went into disrepair, the Nissen huts were vandalised and eventually demolished. Reg Little has long campaigned for better recognition of the radar site. The fruits of his efforts have now become apparent with a notice at Coleton Camp car park and more information at the visitor centre at Froward Point, as well as further information on The National Trust website.

Brownstone Battery at Froward Point – the following is adapted from a booklet written by Mike Ingram who is the local National Trust Area Warden.

Brownstone Battery is a World War II coastal defence position, situated on the eastern side of the mouth of the river Dart estuary at Froward Point. This area has commanding views across Start Bay, which helped in its defence role.

The site consists of two gun batteries, two searchlight positions and a variety of other buildings, including an observation post, generator room, ammunition store, general store and mess rooms, which can still be seen. There were also several buildings to the east of this main group which have since been destroyed, included in this was the accommodation block and latrines.

The area is now owned and managed by The National Trust and is within the Froward Point Site of Special Scientific Interest and Area of Outstanding Natural Beauty. It is accessible from Brownstone car park via a military road, which was built to serve the battery. It is not only important historically but it is one of the few remaining coastal batteries which is largely intact in this country.

Brownstone Battery was built in 1940 as a 'Close Defence Site'. Its function was to engage enemy forces and stop them from landing on Slapton or Blackpool Sands and to destroy any beachhead which the German forces might try to establish. It was known that Hitler had formulated an invasion plan of Britain called Operation Sealion, so there was a real concern of a German land invasion along the South Coast of England. Brownstone Battery was an integral part of the defence strategy of the area. Dartmouth was vulnerable to attack as it is not only a port but was regularly used by the navy and housed a Motor Torpedo Boat installation and anti-submarine nets at the mouth of the estuary. There was also a military boat repairing facility at Philip's Shipyard by Noss Creek.

Dartmouth Castle on the west side of the river had a battery of 4.7inch guns and there was an anti-aircraft gun site on Jawbones Hill behind the town. In addition on the Kingswear side there was a machine gun post at Kingswear Castle and a land based torpedo launching site below Kingswear Court. Dartmouth was bombed on more than one occasion and both the town and Philip's Shipyard suffered considerable damage with loss of life.

Brownstone Battery was manned by approximately 230 soldiers of the 52nd Bedfordshire Yeomanry Regiment between 1940 and 1942, when they were moved to Fleetwood in Lancashire to form a field battery unit. This was due to the arrival of American forces who took over large parts of the Dart and Start Bay area. From 1942 until the end of the war, the Home Guard operated the site under the auspices of the Royal Artillery, but there is little information available for this period.

The Battery was decommissioned in 1956 although the guns were still in place in 1951, as noted from aerial photographs. A caretaker lived on site and looked after the site from the end of the war until the area was returned to the estate of Higher Brownstone in 1956 from whom it was requisitioned. The caretaker and his family lived in one of the Nissan Huts and later became a farm worker at Brownstone.

The National Trust has owned the site since 1982 when it was bought as part of the Enterprise Neptune Campaign to protect unspoilt coastline. At the time of its construction, there was more tree cover with a large part of the area dominated by Monterey and Corsican pines planted in 1904. This no doubt aided concealment of the battery from enemy aircraft and from RAF aerial photographs taken in 1942 it is difficult to pick out the buildings.

The severe storm of January 1990 blew down a large number of mature trees and therefore exposed the site.

The two guns were 6" ex-naval type, thought to have originated from a First World War battleship used in the battle of Jutland in 1916. They had a range of 25,000 yards (14 Miles). However, evidence suggests that these were replaced at a later date during the war with 6" land based guns. Each gun was situated on top of an iron plate which lay over the gun emplacement and was secured onto iron supporting rods, the remains of which are on the bottom of each emplacement. A concrete curtain was built in front of each gun of which only the foundations can now be seen. The guns could be swung 45° in either direction.

Each gun was operated by two teams of thirteen men, i.e. there would be two shifts working and for each team there was one senior NCO and two gun layers who were responsible for the maintenance of the guns.

Number 2 gun position

Any firing of the guns was controlled by the command post at Dartmouth Naval College, which sent radio messages about likely targets to Brownstone Battery. The range and bearings for the firing were worked out in the observation post with the relevant information relayed to the gunners via a tannoy system.

On the order to load, the two gun loaders would load the shell and then the charge. Two more men would set the fuse and when fully loaded the breach would be closed and a firing cartridge inserted (this resembled a .303blank). On the order to fire, a lanyard would be pulled, firing the cartridge which would in turn ignite the charge and thus propel the shell to the designated target. After each firing, the breach would be opened and the loaders would wash out the gun barrel and the mushroom head of the breach before reloading. Approximately four shells could be fired per minute.

The charges for these guns were of two types - either cartridge or cordite. The cartridge was a brass cylinder filled with explosive and the cordite was a silk bag filled with four small bags depending on the range required. For example, for long range three or four bags would be used and for shorter range, one or two bags. Silk was used for the bags so when the gun was fired, the heat would destroy the bag completely, leaving no residue in the breach.

The lower of the two guns (No2 gun) has a miniature railway running down to it from an ammunition store higher up the slope. At the top of the slope, in front of the store, there are cast iron remains of the mountings on which a $1^{1}/2$-hp Lister engine stood. Usually 4-6 shells weighing around 90lbs each were loaded by hand onto a small truck or 'bogey' and freewheeled down to the gun. The engine was used only for bringing the truck back up to the ammunition store. All shells for the number one gun were transported manually from the store.

Railway for transporting ammunition to No2 gun

The recesses around each gun site were used for storing ammunition and originally had steel shutters over them. There is also an access tunnel to the gun mountings for maintenance purposes.

It is thought that the guns were dismantled and taken to Coypool at Plymouth to be sold for scrap, but unsubstantiated local reports suggest that they were thrown into the sea nearby. It is hoped a future diving expedition will confirm this.

A large gorse fire in December 2001 below the gun sites revealed several artefacts from the period the Battery was occupied. Most interesting was the remains of the gun mounting from number two gun which can be seen below the emplacement. It appears that there was an attempt to roll the mounting down the cliffs and into the sea. When it failed to go the full distance, efforts were apparently made to break it up, probably using explosives as only half this cast iron mounting remains and there are several large pieces of it scattered around the site.

It is likely that the mounting for number two gun was rolled off its emplacement and may well be in the sea, as no remains were found below its position. Also found were a set of wheels from the "bogey" or trolley which took the shells down the miniature railway from the ammunition store to number two gun.

Each of the guns had a searchlight close to the high water mark on the cliffs. Each of these had a 26" (66.04cm)-carbon arc projector and was manned by two teams of five who worked in shifts, as with the gun positions. A flight of steps with iron railings leads down to the searchlights and this had to be maintained to prevent vegetation encroachment, so quick and easy access to the searchlights could be had particularly at night.

Searchlight position on the Dart estuary

Below the searchlight batteries the whole cliff area was covered in barbed wire which was laid by the soldiers. Local rumour has suggested that the searchlights were thrown into the sea after the war and, as with the guns, a future diving expedition might confirm this.

The crew for the searchlight battery used building No 7 as a stand down hut. This building was only discovered during a survey in 1994, as it was largely covered in undergrowth. There was an intact stove inside but unfortunately has since been vandalised.

The Generator Sheds
Only generator shed number 9 can be viewed inside, through the iron grills, and this served Number 1 searchlight. The generator in building number 4 served Number 2 searchlight and the needs of the rest of the battery. Nothing is known of the generator types or specifications.

Several people worked in The Battery Observation Post (B.O.P) including signallers, telephonists, radio control, gun control officers and clerks. A concrete pillar inside, originally held a bearing plate for a depression range finder (DRF) and there was also a chart table which folded down from the wall. The iron shutters fold down. There are reinforced glass windows beneath which can be opened. Vandalism over the years has unfortunately destroyed much of what was left in this building. The grass area behind the observation building used for drill was kept mown and the three concrete blocks to the left of the observation building are thought to have supported an aerial mast.

The shells and cordite were kept separately in Ammunition Stores and the storage racks can be seen in the buildings.

The remainder of the buildings were a number of mostly corrugated Nissen huts to the east of the main group, housing regular soldiers. There were also latrines and washrooms, evidence of which, such as clay pipes and drains, can be found in places. This area is now largely covered in scrub. Water for the site was piped down from a 10,000-gallon header tank near what is now Brownstone car park. This fed into a smaller tank, the supports of which can be seen just inside the gateway on the left, as you enter the Battery from the military road.

References:
World War II database at ww2db.com
Mike Ingram of The National Trust
Reg Little
Mike and Andrew Passmore have written a very comprehensive book titled 'RAF Air Defence Radar Stations in Devon'

17. Finale

Reg Little in his 'Growing up in Wartime Kingswear' reflects that:

'Many other people will have many other memories of wartime Kingswear and Dartmouth. Mine are the still vivid memories of a 12 -18 year old who was greatly involved in the combined effort made by one and all in a time of great national emergency. What a pity that more of this spirit does not seem to exist in the present day'

It has been a great privilege to have been able to talk to so many people and tap into their experiences and I am very grateful to them for their kindness in allowing me to do so.

If this book has achieved nothing else, I hope that it allows some of the often vivid memories of these folks to be preserved.